CW00432417

Recovery from the Deluge of Time

By Jennifer Kendrick

Edited by Patricia Main BA(Hons) MA

(c) Jennifer Kendrick 2021

All rights reserved to Jennifer Kendrick. This book or any portion thereof may not be reproduced or used in any manner whatsoever without the express written permission of the author except for the use of brief quotations in a book review.

About the author.....

Jennifer Kendrick was born and grew up in Weston-super-Mare. She qualified as a general nurse in the 1950's in Kent before training and working in plastic surgery at East Grinstead. Then marriage and a move to Sierra Leone, West Africa followed by three children and a busy family life all over the UK.

After many years in the School Health Service specialising in enuresis, Jennifer retired in 1997 and settled, very happily, in Dursley.

Contents

Personalities

Memories are made of this ...

"Sometimes I just sits and thinks and sometimes I just sits! My beloved Granny used to say as I cuddled up to her for quiet times. She was always there with elastic arms and an infectious giggle that made her eyes sparkle and her ample bosoms wobble. I pray that one day my grand-daughter, Kayleigh, will have happy memories of our time together.

Marnie and Pamp – My Bristol Granny and Grandpa

We were a very busy family and I was only too pleased to be the back-up crew as my three children and their father went car racing, motor cycling, gliding, parachuting, diving and numerous expeditions! Once I had seen to their physical needs and nourishment, I was content to be a camp follower or stay at home to knit, crochet, sew and cook, hoping and praying they would come back safely and looking forward to hearing all about their escapades. Sitting and thinking was not an easy option.

One Christmas I proudly presented my two teenage girls with embroidered pictures I had made during the year. They were thrilled but I sensed my son's disappointment and he made it very clear that he was upset that he did not get one. It never occurred to me! How sexist! I was sad and sat down to think.

A few months went by and his 18th birthday loomed large. I thanked God that he had survived, relatively unscathed, all the alarms and exertions of growing up and that we had a good relationship, but what on earth could I give him to celebrate his coming of age?

Not long afterwards, I went to my busy cupboard and found a plastic bag. Inside were bits and pieces of material which I did not recognise but looked interesting enough for the housework to be immediately abandoned. In no time and with no effort I had assembled a perfect resemblance of Neil's black and white cat complete with bright orange backing and a suitable frame. It was a miracle.

More than 20 years on, and that picture has travelled many miles, hung in an assortment of lodgings and apartments but now has pride of place in Neil's permanent home as he pursues a career teaching design and technology. I, meanwhile, have the time and inclination to sit and think, and constantly thank God for His wonderful ways and the memories.

Songs of Praise

At St. Marks Church, we were asked to choose hymns for our very own Songs of Praise. For me this was easy, as from all the lovely music and words, both ancient and modern, there is one that is my all-time favourite.

During the dark and difficult days of the war, my mother was very ill following a devastating stillbirth and was often in hospital. When my father was posted abroad in the RAF, my brother and I went to live with my grandparents. I was 6 years old, and thought that we were being evacuated for safety reasons and clutched my gas mask and teddy bear, feeling quite important and excited by the move. In retrospect, of course, I realise how sheltered I was from the real truth and am thankful.

My Granny Marney was a wonderful person. She had twinkling eyes, a whiskery chin that tickled you, ample bosoms that wobbled when she laughed and elastic arms that gathered up as many of her grandchildren as were around her at any one time. Her legs were cruelly crippled by arthritis so she always wore long floaty skirts and her large lap was like a hammock where I loved to sit and be cuddled, especially when we were in the cupboard under the stairs during the frequent air raids. She never seemed upset or worried even when bombs dropped close by and we had narrow escapes. She often sang "Thine Forever, God of Love" and I was sure that whatever happened to us, we were all in safe keeping. Those cherished memories have stood me in good stead over the years. May they comfort others too.

Thine for ever! God of love,
Hear us from thy throne above;
Thine for ever may we be
Here and in eternity.

Thine for ever! O how blest
They who find in thee their rest!
Saviour, guardian, heavenly friend
O defend us to the end.

Thine for ever! Lord of life,
Shield us through our earthly strife;
Though the Life, the Truth, the Way,
Guide us to the realms of day.

Thine for ever! Shepherd, keep
Us thy frail and trembling sheep;
Safe alone beneath they car,
Let us all thy goodness share.

Thine for ever! Thou our guide,
All our wants by thee supplied,
All our sins by thee forgiven,
Lead us, Lord, form earth to heaven.

Jennifer and Granddaughter K.J.

God Bless Grannies

I was a very lucky little girl and had two devoted Grannies. Marney, my Bristol Granny was round and bouncy with enormous bosoms that wobbled when she laughed, elastic arms that enveloped me in cosy cuddles, a whiskery chin that tickled and eyes that sparkled like jewels in the sun. Her poor body was racked by arthritis making mobility a problem, but her lap was an oasis of calm and when the adult world seemed an alien and scary place, she sang "Thine For Ever" as she rocked me gently to sleep. She lived modestly in a little house with an ever-open door where all comers were welcome any time. We had such fun.

By contrast, my Canterbury Granny was a Queen Mary look-alike, slim and upright with elegant outfits, attended Church regularly and gave the distinct impression that she had a hot line to God! Her long grey hair, immaculately scraped back in a bun, enhanced her beautiful complexion and even when I once saw her with plaits, she still exuded a slightly distant air of grace and deportment.

My Canterbury Granny

Her house was very grand, approached by a gravel drive to an enormous oak door with great big black studs which I thought was a portcullis entrance to a castle! Inside, the huge hall boasted a sweeping staircase which divided as it swept up to the landing and umpteen bedrooms. Downstairs, a diminutive live-in housekeeper addressed me as "Miss Jennifer", cooked delicious food in a kitchen the size of a hockey pitch, and waited on us in the grand oak panelled dining room. I loved being treated like a princess but sensed that such a lifestyle had some constraints. Quite used to the austerity of wartime, I was not an acquisitive child and accepted the grand surroundings as a museum piece, but there was one large picture that I coveted. Pretty in shades of pale blue and green and painted by Margaret Tarrant whose illustrations in my first Bible were such a joy, it portrayed the Madonna in a field of lilies, with the infant Jesus on her shoulder.

I was about ten years old and we visited Granny, now confined to bed and frail. Her changed condition worried me but there was still that picture on the wall assuring me that some things remain constant. Mindful of good manners, I waited patiently for a break in the adult conversation and then politely addressed my question:

"Please Granny, when you are dead and don't need that picture any more, may I have it?"

I was stunned by the palpable change in the atmosphere as there was a collective intake of adult breath and all eyes focused on me in disbelief. What had I done? I don't remember what happened next, but in my teens I inherited that wonderful picture, of no great monetary value but to me the most treasured possession and absolutely priceless. Sadly, some time later it was stolen in a burglary and over the intervening years has proved impossible to replace. I have had to learn to live with the loss but am ever hopeful I shall find it again some day.

THE LILIES OF THE FIELD

by

Margaret W. Tarrant

My Grannies were so different but equally influential in my life and I am thankful for their example and those precious memories which are quite safe form thieving hands.

Praise to the Holiest

We were a diverse group of ladies out to lunch and a spot of early Christmas shopping. In a quiet moment one of them asked me about the prayer that Christians say about being like lost sheep, sorry for things left undone and things done that ought not to have been done ... I said I thought she meant the General Confession and was sure, given time, I could find a copy for her.

The dark drive back in the rainy rush-hour put all thoughts out of my mind, so imagine my surprise when I walked into my house and without thinking, went straight to the bookcase. There, like a beacon, was my Book of Common Prayer, a Confirmation present to me fifty years ago, beautifully bound in white with gold leaf, showing healthy signs of shabbiness due to age and regular use. I felt the Lord telling me that this was the book to give away and sadly set it on one side while I cooked my supper. Later, I picked it up, wondering what on earth I would do without it and not at all sure I wanted to part with it.

Next morning, I was prompted to open a drawer in my desk which is seldom visited and found another Book of Common Prayer that had been a Christmas present to me sixty-seven years ago from my beloved Granny – she of the giant lap, elastic arms, wobbly bosom, twinkly eyes and whiskery chin! Smothered in my Brownie badges, a victim of poor storage and years of neglect, I felt a sense of wonder at this find. As I held it, it fell open at an illustration by Margaret Tarrant of Mary in a field of lilies with Baby Jesus on her shoulder, a large copy of which always hung on my other Granny's bedroom wall. I always loved it and when she died I inherited this precious picture and treasured it for ages until it was stolen in a burglary.

For more than twenty-five years I had made repeated attempts to replace it without success, and only recently thought I had managed it, when the firm's London office was damaged by floods and my quest came to an abrupt end yet again. I am not good at letting go and letting God, but am truly thankful He never gives up on me.

No doubt, over all that time, He has been desperately disappointed as He tried to help me find that picture in that book in the drawer. So near, and yet so far!

At last, I was obedient and have that picture and all those happy memories restored to me. Needless to say, the lady concerned was absolutely thrilled with the other book and promised to treasure it for ever.

Praise to the Holiest in the heights
And in the depths be praise.
In all His works most wonderful,
Most sure in all his ways.

Family Resolution

My mother-in-law was, at one time, a renowned opera singer, no doubt about it. In Joyce Grenfell's immortal words, she was like a galleon on full sail. Her well-upholstered chest resembled a spinnaker inflated by a gently following breeze and a disapproving look from her penetrating hazel eyes was enough to bring down an Exocet missile. She lived with her devoted, quiet and charismatic husband in a large semi-detached house in a genteel suburb of Sevenoaks. Furnished a bit like a museum with huge chunks of dark oak from floor to ceiling, the gloom was lifted by light coloured chintz furnishings and white carpets on which, even without shoes or barefoot straight from the bath, I seemed to leave marks. Not good, especially when you are the chosen one of the only son amongst several impressive daughters and desperate to impress! She was a formidable bridge player and even seasoned participants could be reduced to trembling wrecks by an unwise move. As someone who was always beaten at cards, even in a solo game of patience, I was already a lost cause. Her kitchen boasted the very latest and, to me, totally baffling gadgets that whizzed and sliced and chopped and mixed at the touch of a button. The secret, of course, was in the programming which I never mastered, so after a few false starts - one which ended in decorating the ceiling with raw cake mix – I was, forever, excused all culinary duties in her house.

Somehow, I managed to survive a prolonged apprenticeship as a prospective spouse to her precious son and, mercifully, our early married life was spent in the totally inaccessible far-flung outpost of Sierra Leone, completely devoid of any mod cons or means of communication. Then remote parts of Northern England beckoned which were difficult to reach without a car.

Having three children in three years required my total commitment and managing on a tight budget was a full-time occupation which left little time for anything else. To me it was sheer joy, and oh so simple with priorities being to put food on the table, provide plenty of clean clothes and have lots of fun. The garden was somewhere to hang the washing and play jungle games amongst the neglected vegetation, whilst the house was a shelter where writing "I love you" in the dust was more appealing than dirtying a cloth moving it somewhere else.

Visitors were always welcomed, but when the in-laws were due it was particularly challenging as chaos was dutifully reined in to resemble order. I remember vividly once when they were there and a very dear bachelor friend of ours appeared unannounced, driving an amazing sports car. He had been working abroad and out of touch for some time, so the element of surprise and delight were intoxicating and the somewhat subdued atmosphere suddenly became frenetic. For a few hours we had a ball. Then, later that evening, our visitor having left to catch up with other friends, the children exhausted and tucked up in bed, and our menfolk content to retire with pipe tobacco, a noggin and the newspaper to another room, my mother-in-law found the opportunity to hold court. With no preamble and only me to address, she slowly and deliberately announced in full voice: "The time has come, my dear, for you to act with a modicum of decorum!" which took me a while to digest and translate as "grow up and stop being so scatty!" Short, sharp and to the point, it made a great impression but not a lot immediately changed. Eventually, after many months and much thought, I was brave enough to take the initiative. I began by suggesting that we both had a vested interest in the well-being of all members of the family, but different management skills and priorities and perhaps we needed a compromise. To my surprise she readily agreed and we both relaxed and discussed things at great length. From then on, she accepted that my chaotic household was actually clean enough to be healthy and I made sure that when we visited her there were no crumbs on the carpet or dirty marks on the wall when we left. Everyone lived happy ever after and I shall always be grateful for her understanding and wise counsel. Even when she died aged 90, she was still Duchess to us all.

Northfield Cottage

Sitting in the Captain's chair at the beginning of the day
It's raining hard, the clouds are low, there's glory in the grey.
Sitting in the Captain's chair, the next day after noon
The sun shines from a clear blue sky, ducks swim on the lagoon.
Sitting in the Captain's chair at the ending of the day
The wind blows fluffy clouds about. I'm glad I'm here today.

Sitting in the Captain's chair on a very different day
Stark warnings of a hurricane that's hastening our way.
Sitting in the Captain's chair I watch the trees bend prone.
The east wind whistles like a witch, that crow could be a crone!
What joy to have a seat to watch the natural world unfurled
Dark and light, dull and bright, it's plain and then it's purled.

Ode to Cousin Jo

Jo and I shared great-grannies so were sort of cousins. By accident of birth, we descended from the WINDMILL dynasty, late of Knowle in Bristol and especially a long line of strong women which we seem to have perpetuated. Sadly, the family name has all but disappeared as the legion of menfolk failed to reproduce direct heirs. We were friends and allies through the best of times and the worst of times, particularly when we shared the care of another distant Windmill cousin who had no close family, so as she steadily declined into dementia, Jo and I became her formidable and determined advocates ensuring her end of life was dignified, stimulating and comfortable.

The summer of 2010 found us on holiday on Exmoor, not an area we had ever visited. I had bravely bitten the bullet, tackled the bewildering internet and booked what appeared to be an idyllic B&B, and surprisingly cheap. In fact, the farm was so well hidden we had to abandon the car, climb through dense undergrowth, cross a rickety bridge and gingerly climb a crumbling wooden staircase to reach the rather forbidding front door. On the way, we noticed chickens that even the fox had deemed inedible, push-me-pull-you sheep that looked like walking hearth rugs and tripod dogs of all shapes and sizes as well as other four-legged animals of dubious origin, age and species. We were warmly welcomed by a Hobbit, characteristically short and shrivelled who summoned his wife, a giant with a lawyer's bearing and a voice to match. The place was dusty and dark, but in the gloom we could vaguely identify antique Great Western Railway paraphernalia so abundant there was no space to sit and little room to move. We were speechless for once but there was no turning back. After a day's driving that covered less than 100 miles, mostly through narrow winding lanes that lacked signposts and, as the sun was setting, we were already contemplating camping in the hedgerow. In the end, we found the food was interesting and edible, the water brown but drinkable and the beds sparkly clean and comfortable. We stayed three nights and gathered much material for amusing anecdotes.

Christmas 2012 saw us declare liberation and independence, politely but firmly refusing all other offers, as we booked into a motel on a busy motorway roundabout at Tamworth for the festive season. Lichfield Cathedral was a joy and a visit to the nearby National Arboretum ticked another box on our bucket list, whilst a friendly canal-side pub was a great source of social gathering and yummy food. One very dark, wet and windy night we inadvertently strayed into an industrial estate and got locked in when the barriers closed behind us. We eventually escaped, only, once again, to get lost in a maze of narrow anonymous country lanes with absolutely no point of reference except the roar of the nearby motorway. After careful consideration, we accepted defeat and phoned Jo's daughter, Clare, who, like Merlin the magician without a sat. nav., discovered our whereabouts and duly delivered us back to our base.

We always had fun whenever we were together. Even in our mid-seventies, heaving huge boulders and shovelling mountains of earth to reduce the size of the pond in her large garden made us ache with giggles, not the physical effort, and we were wise enough to make a little album of fuzzy photos to remind us of what had achieved despite advancing years.

.

Cousin Jo and Jennifer: Pond builders

We played Pooh Sticks on the bridge over the little stream at Publow in Somerset, as we had done many times before over the decades. Though more hazardous due to our lack of agility, it was no less competitive, and it is there that we scattered her ashes and gave thanks. I miss her, but memories need not fade and I am glad she is at peace.

Understanding

The last few weeks have been a struggle of fear and foreboding. Sufficient to say that, far away in Australia, my beloved, middle-aged son's life has turned upside down as his marriage ended, leaving him heart-broken, homeless and humiliated. Mercifully, his sister was able to fly 1,000 miles from Sydney to Brisbane (it's a huge country) to be a comfort and support, and his countless friends have rallied round with practical solutions. Nevertheless, there was nothing I could do to ease his hurt as I used to when he was a little boy when we managed everything with footballer's cream and "Puff the magic powder". I have never doubted the power of positive thinking and my faith has never wavered so I did not hesitate to ask for prayer support and immediately felt stronger when the mist began to clear and a future seemed possible.

My son is a character who eventually found his calling, after many false starts in a variety of jobs in the UK from seaman to working in a tyre factory; scene shifter to motor cycle courier to name but a few. Well over 30, he went to university to train as a teacher and after a few years, emigrated to further his career concentrating on difficult young people and enjoying success where others had often failed. He was offered a challenge to move to BAMAGA in remote North Queensland to teach in a college where English is the second language and the needs of inspirational leaders a priority.

Desperately in need of a new start, and with all his life experiences, practical skills, charisma, charm and humility, it seemed tailor-made. Today my Bible fell open at Psalm 119 vv 33-40, a prayer for understanding.

Then, way out of my comfort zone, as I made preparation to lead the Women's World Day of Prayer service, a scrappy bit of paper appeared with words from Colin Urquhart's "When the Spirit Comes" which caused more pause for thought ...

I, the Lord, promise to lead you in all things. To enrich greatly your lives with many blessings, if only you will be faithful to me, I will enter into an agreement with you, an agreement which I will honour because of my love for you. You are to be concerned with the spreading of my word of truth in this parish. You are to show the quality of love I require of my children to Christians in other churches. Let no-one be afraid, as by doing this you will be closer to me in love.

There is no doubt in my mind that all this is not simply coincidence, but that God is at work in his mysterious way. As the storm clouds of sadness and anxiety gradually start to lift and I hear the still, small voice murmur gentle reassurance that all will be well, I am truly thankful.

A Good Shepherd

My brother, Brian, was a remarkable man. Four years my senior, he was gifted academically, a fine sportsman, artistic, a model son and definitely the apple of my mother's eye. After a brilliant career at Oxford, he won a coveted scholarship to Harvard and then went on to study at the Sorbonne in Paris. Back in Oxford again, he graduated in all the Slav languages and it was no surprise that in 1956 he went to Hungary as part of the British Aid project. Without warning he returned some months later with a refugee he had rescued from torture and smuggled into my parents' house in Kent. To their eternal credit, they were quite unfazed and life caried on as normal.

Everything changed quite suddenly in 1960 when, following the sudden death of our beloved father, Brian collapsed and was diagnosed as suffering rom a virulent form of pulmonary TB. For nearly 2 years he was isolated in a small room in a Swiss sanatorium with minimal visits with other people whilst contact with the outside world was limited to the view from a tiny window in his single cell. He reminded me of John Bunyan.

Physically diminished but still with determination and needing the pure fresh mountain air to help his recovery, once he was discharged, he stayed in the area and did a course in animal husbandry, finding a special interest in sheep management. Eventually, and for more than 25 years he spent weeks at a time high up in the Alps on his own with his dog with sole responsibility for the welfare of a large flock. He settled in a village restoring an ancient stone cottage and was active in the locality. With his flowing black cloak in winter, long hair and bushy beard, he was well known and highly respected for his wisdom, compassion and commitment to the well-being of our world and everything in it, animal, vegetable or mineral. Sometimes controversial, he led from the front, listening to all and sundry, and with discernment he seemed to know when to shake the dust from his heels and move on. He died too soon but his memory lives on and to those of us who knew and loved him, he will always be our good shepherd.

Loving and Letting Go

My children had a good relationship with my mother. During the war she, like millions of others had kept the home fires burning. That meant living day to day with little money, clothes and food rationing and facing an uncertain future. I grew up thinking her distant and difficult, but in retrospect, maybe she was simply focused on our survival, and missing my dad who was away in the Forces. To my brother and me, life was an exciting adventure, with time spent in our Morrison shelter while air raids raged roundabout, and then treasure hunts for shrapnel souvenirs and bits of burnt parachute after the bombers had gone. We escaped serious mishaps or injuries and my dad eventually came home safely.

In 1961, as a young widow who had not had the opportunity to work since her marriage, she faced life alone, and took full advantage of the fledgling Women's Lib movement, emerging like a butterfly from a chrysalis! She had always been practical and thrifty with 'make do and mend' producing all sorts of outfits from anything available. Gradually, with the advent of new materials and patterns, she modestly created more, tastefully embellished them with costume jewellery and wore just enough make-up to be smart. She took on various voluntary roles, a part-time paid job as a doctor's receptionist, joined local organisations and learnt to drive.

The world was still a largely unexplored planet and travel only open to those with a lot of cash or by staying at home reading books from the library and dreaming dreams. My mum was determined and single-minded enough to find a way of getting round such difficulties and discovered a trip on a banana boat sailing out of Avonmouth to the West Indies, was possible and, with very basic accommodation, and facilities affordable. That was just the start and she spent the next few years sailing round the world on various cargo ships and crossing continents on less than reliable transport with total strangers. Only communication was ship to shore radio in emergencies (we got a vague message that she was adrift on a burning ship one dark night) so months went by when we had no idea where she was, but presumed she was still alive.

By the time my three children were old enough to be interested in their "galloping granny's" travels she was safely shore-based and anchored in Dartmouth with uninterrupted views of the river and close encounters with marine life of all kinds. My son, in particular, loved staying with her and never tired of hearing tales of life on the ocean waves, but aged six, caused a major incident when he just disappeared. After hours of frantic searching, he was discovered desperately trying to persuade a local ship's crew that he would be a great asset to their workforce! Only two years later he had helped build himself a dinghy and from then on spent all school holidays afloat.

Towards the end of her life, my mother considerately decluttered her home and shared a mountain of memorabilia, which included arts and needlecrafts she had done in every medium and are still in our possession. My youngest daughter particularly treasured a ring that was part of her legacy. Not valuable or sparkly or even pretty, but something Granny always wore, just a large, oval blue polished pebble in a silver setting which Frankie only took off to go to school where uniform rules were strict. One summer she lost it whilst on the beach in Cornwall and we were all heartbroken. Search parties over days failed to find it and our journey back to Birmingham at the end of the holiday was gloomy. Weeks later it was returned by a family of strangers who had been beach combing and remembered seeing a faded note in the village post office asking for help in finding it. Naturally, it became all the more precious, and my daughter was amazingly stoical when, many years later, it was stolen in a burglary ... in Africa! Well-travelled, much loved, but there is a time to let go of belongings and people, and be content with memories which can last forever.

Earliest Childhood Memories

Born in Weston-super-Mare in 1937, my earliest memories are splintered with war-time experiences and an overall feeling of being permanently invincible and independent.

My parents, Frank and Hildegarde Featherstone, were married in 1932 and my brother, Brian, was born a year later. We lived in a very comfortable new-build semi in Farm Road that my father, whilst hailing from Kent and of a very modest income as a commercial traveller, had managed to buy. I don't remember anything prior to him joining up to serve in the Forces, but he was initially based at RAF Locking, which was not far down the road. He used to bring other airmen home for occasional breaks and home cooking and I loved the attention from these glamorous chaps in uniform. They happily allowed themselves to be my patients (I already knew I would be a nurse!) and I annoyed my mother by ripping up precious sheets to make bandages for their pretend injuries. It was all most exciting!

Everything changed dramatically one day as I was clutching my shopping basket at the local greengrocers, and heard grown-ups talking agitatedly about "the invasion". Thinking this was good news, I rushed home to tell my mum but found her most unresponsive which was a huge disappointment and I sulked in my room, gazing out of my window at the far distant hills, waiting for knights in shining armour to appear and take me away to the Land of Green Ginger. Bearing in mind there was very little in the way of news broadcasting or any other communication, so much of what we heard was by word of mouth and not reliable, and it seemed that nothing much happened, except that my father and his friends were no longer visiting but had been posted somewhere far away. I found that most interesting, imagining them in parcels on a magic mission to that land of mystery and intrigue. My mother was not impressed and became detached so we rarely spoke and I was quite content to roam alone in Ashcombe Park having adventures, or in my room dreaming dreams as six-year-olds do.

What I did not realise was that my mother was pregnant, ill and depressed. There was no NHS and very little in the way of support as everybody was busy just trying to survive the austerity, never mind the bombing raids that were increasingly threatening and unpredictable. In retrospect, I understand that she was formidable given the circumstances and, as we saw a German plane in flames pass over our house and crash, clearly remember her lack of emotion, whilst assuring me that all was well, was commendable.

Then suddenly my brother and I landed in Bristol, to be with my maternal grandparents, aunt and uncle, and cousins all together with our rabbit, Jenks, in a three bed house. I didn't appreciate sharing anything, not having a bedroom all to myself and not being free to roam despite Redcatch Park being on the doorstep. I was difficult and demanding, rude and uncooperative, sensing the despair that seeped into every corner of the place and enjoying the fact that I was largely responsible. My granny did her very best, her elastic arms held me close and snuggled into her bosom that smelled of lavender, I felt loved, but it was not enough. My brother pleaded with me to be nice, but I was not interested and went on being disruptive.

Then out of the blue one day, I saw my beloved Daddy walking up the road, so smart in his uniform and clutching a parcel. I remember the slippers he brought me, that were probably plain and simple but felt like Cinderella's sparkly dancing shoes. I remember he took me on a bus into Park Street in Bristol city centre, to Hort's restaurant to have lunch. I was about six years old but knowing that as money was short, I should choose something cheap (not that there was much on the menu) and right at the bottom was Tripe and Onions. Absolutely yummy, I remember every mouthful and feeling special and spoiled. Then my Daddy explained that Mummy was extremely ill in hospital and it was my job to be useful at home to allow him to be away helping to win the war. I don't remember being a model child all of a sudden, but I do remember beginning to understand that we all matter to each other and we all have a responsibility to one another.

It transpired that my mother had had a stillbirth and her health never fully recovered. There was no bereavement counselling and I struggled for years with feelings of resentment at not having a sister, mixed with relief that once my Daddy was home at the end of the war, I was still his only, much-loved daughter, although I have since wondered if I had any other siblings somewhere in Europe. He was special. I remember him still.

A Lasting Legacy of Tough Love

I was probably about eight years old, polite and genteel, sheltered from the rough and tumble of the outside world by a mother determined that I should be raised as a 'little lady'. Despite the austerity of war-time Britain, I was acutely aware of being smartly dressed in outfits which she skilfully crafted from second-hand clothes and my well-groomed hair was always rinsed in camomile to make it shine. I was never allowed to play with the neighbour's children so happily disappeared on my own over the garden fence into the adjacent park, usually with a proper tennis racket and ball whilst the others were together having fun playing in the road with chalk and sticks and home-made toys.

A few doors away lived an old lady who, if truth be told, frightened me a lot, so I decided to dislike her. Stooped and slightly built, with a shuffling gait aided by a gnarled walking stick, she would take a few short, slow steps, stop for breath and look around. Her grey crinkled hair matched her grey wrinkled face, topped by a strange floppy hat and punctuated by a menacing grin revealing sharp, yellowy, misshapen fangs that, despite black gaping spaces, would probably eat anything and could certainly crush bones. After careful consideration, I invented a game to pass the time when I had to stay home. Very simply, it involved standing on the window sill waiting for 'Winnie Peg' to pass by and silently making rude faces as she stood and stared, open-mouthed. It was my secret, great fun and made us equal – or so I thought.

Then one day, as I happily set off through the garden gate to go to the park, I was approached by a funny little man in a trilby hat and cream-coloured raincoat who, whilst still some way off, wagged his finger at me. He was clearly very cross but, remembering my manners, I stood my ground to hear what he had to say. He was short, with steel-rimmed spectacles perched on the end of his hooked nose, a sharp pointy chin, thin lips and a little voice.

"If you don't stop insulting my wife, I shall have you taken away by PC Pokeman," he squeaked.

I was pretty sure that our local bobby was a friend who would not have anything to do with this man, so I went straight home to sort things out. It just so happened that my adored Daddy was on embarkation leave from the RAF. Grown-ups talked of imminent invasion which sounded important so I knew there was no time to lose. Straightaway, I asked if somebody could be taken away by the police for pulling funny faces at a passer-by from behind a window. His reaction was measured and firm as he gently enquired who I had upset. It was a mystery how he connected me with my secret, unseemly conduct, but I knew my cover was blown.

My father, my brother and me, 1943

I learnt a lot that day, especially that honesty is the best policy, but above all that I was blessed with an earthly father who closely resembled my juvenile image of Him in Heaven. Understanding, patient, kind, caring and forgiving BUT equally capable of stern admonishment and retribution when justice was required. I was given a suitable sanction. Tough love is a priceless gift that sets you free. I had lots of that and am deeply grateful.

'Til All our Strivings Cease

I have just been changing the duvet cover on my bed. If only someone would invent a machine to do the job or at least give me elastic arms to save me struggling. That set me thinking about all the hospital beds I made as a student nurse. Always two of us, everything to hand and the linen and blankets on the bed carefully measured so that the patients were comfortable and ship-shape for Matron's round.

Arriving for my first day on the ward, keen to please Sister who had a reputation as a battleaxe, I was sent to make a bed ... oh, so simple! Even on my own I did it quickly and was soon back to ask Sister for a more demanding task. To my surprise she swept down the ward like a ship in full sail to inspect my handiwork. I waited for praise to be heaped on my young shoulders but instead she picked up the pillow, shook it under my nose and demanded to know "What is THIS?" I felt confused and tried to satisfy her, all to no avail. Eventually it transpired that there were dog-ears on the pillow slip where the pillow had not reached the corners.

"Do it PROPERLY" still rings in my ears. She was a hard task master and I learned over the years that "no comment" was as near praise as she ever gave, but this did not stop me trying and in so doing, gained experience and confidence that I was able to share and pass on to others as time went by. When I was a patient on the same ward, I could see how she trusted and relied on her team and their training which left her free to minister to those in her care who needed reassurance, hope and love, and the strength to cope with fear pain and sometimes death. At the same time, she was always available to her staff whether junior and needing lots of guidance or more senior and ready to accept greater responsibility.

It makes me think of how we are with God. As baby Christians we learn a little and think we know the lot. He has to work patiently with gentle firmness to make us accept his teaching, essential for moving on effectively. Sometimes it is a lonely path as He allows us the freedom to practice alone. This leaves Him more time to devote to others, and us to be more independent. Have faith that He is never far away. "No comment" may be just His way of saying "You're doing OK".

Joyful Reunion

There was something different about her as she wandered aimlessly round the playground of that inner city secondary school. As the School Nurse, I was responsible for their health and welfare and often picked up useful information by chance encounters, so made mental notes. Her shoulders were rounded, she dragged her feet, her long black hair looked dull and her pale face had a haunted look … but she was beautiful.

Over the following many months I saw her more often as she came to the Medical Room with minor complaints and I knew for certain that there was something seriously amiss. Eventually she confessed – she was being sexually abused by her father. Sworn to secrecy, she felt guilty and totally responsible.

The immediate aftermath of this confession is blurred in my memory as so much agony, anger, misery and desolation had to be carefully dealt with. Despite everything, when the case came to court, she withdrew all allegations. It was a sad day.

This poor tormented child tried to commit suicide and I arranged for her to be admitted to an adolescent unit in the local Hospital as a place of safety. Immediately she refused all food and her condition rapidly deteriorated. One day in desperation, I gathered her lifeless body roughly in my arms, told her how much I loved her and prayed for peace for her.

All that happened a long time ago. She is now a tall, elegant even more beautiful young lady, married, full of confidence and sure of her future. Nothing can make up for the childhood she was so cruelly denied, but I thank God for His divine intervention when all human endeavour was exhausted.

God is Everywhere

It had been a very busy few weeks of essential and enjoyable events when Saturday dawned, gently easing me into a day with a distinct nip of Autumn in the air. I had the choice of joining friends at a coffee concert but decided to stay home and, as I sat quietly at my desk with my mind in neutral, the telephone rang with a request to write something about God and surprises.

I took in every detail of my pretty little garden which is, to me, a jungle of joy. There are lots of pretty plants, many that are weeds to the purists. I have no room for dandelions and am fed up with other people's cats, but slugs, snails, caterpillars and all manner of other creeping things which are a pain to proper growers are OK by me because they happen in God's wonderful world as if by chance. Bees buzz and birds splash about in the bath, before retiring to a convenient bush to twitter excitedly making me smile. Then silence and a moment for thought, presently interrupted by intermittent sounds of traffic, a small plane doing breath-taking aerobatics and neighbours chatting. Then silence again. Not even a rustle of wind to disturb the total silence and absolute peace. How does all this happen? Why? Are we surprised? How often do we notice such things? Do we care?

As I sit quietly, I remember my late, lamented, greatly loved and respected Godmother who was a constant source of spiritual inspiration throughout my life until she died twenty years ago, aged ninety. When I was a little girl she used to appear, as if by magic, at the railway station, emerging form the smoky haze of the giant steam train like an ethereal being from a heavenly kingdom. A slightly slimmer, taller version of Margaret Rutherford, she had pretty white hair, a wobbly double chin and untethered bosom, a booming voice, wonderfully floaty clothes and a commanding presence that demanded attention, spelt wisdom and assurance, kindness and caring all at once. A sort of God's messenger with surprises in her suitcase. There were no phones so letters were our only direct source of communication when she was elsewhere, but we had a special bond through prayer and our very own private personal triumvirate of Me, Her and Him which never failed. Amazing!

Recently I have been struggling for several weeks to know how to contact someone who has lost his wife to whom he was utterly devoted, despite the Alzheimer's Disease which had engulfed her for many years. Daily I tried to write a note of condolence, but no words came and the telephone was definitely a non-starter. I did so want to let him know how sad I was for him, though not sorry her strife on earth was over. I felt a sense of emptiness and failure in my feeble attempt at outreach as time went by with no resolution in sight and I was stumped. Then, in an unexpected place, at an unexpected time, I suddenly bumped into him. The words flowed freely between us without fear or favour and I felt free to give him a hug in the street as a sign of God's love, perfect timing, understanding and compassion.

If we just slow down, we can make room for revelations, hear His voice, deal with stress and uncertainty and find that anything is possible with God, especially when we least expect it. We need not be busy doing things all the time. Simply being can be enough. Being simple, even better.

Surprise! Surprise!

Wisdom

The question is who was the wisest person in my life, and without a doubt I say my sainted, much loved, greatly respected spinster Godmother, Phyllis

Newman, long since departed but always on my mind. For many years she played the rather battered and wheezy organ in her local Cornwall village church, with as much devotion as anyone in a Cathedral.

In retrospect I know very little about her origins or life except that she and my parents, long before they married, were members of a Tennis Club in Bristol in the 1920s. She was an abiding influence, present or not, from my earliest memory as a small child to the day she died, aged 90. I remember her as sage, knowing, understanding, informed, shrewd, discerning, prudent, judicious, interesting, gentle and firm. Above all, she showed me tough love.

Close to six feet tall and well built, there was nothing remotely feminine about her as in the days of nipped-in waists and slender hips, she refused to be corseted, so bosoms bounced unrestrained, shapeless floaty skirts reached her ankles and big feet were vaguely housed in heavy, flat, brown leather Jesus sandals. Not pretty, but with a flawless complexion, her wavy hair, usually collar length, was carelessly coiffed with a brush and shone like sun on snow. She spoke deliberately in a deep voice, with every syllable carefully crafted which made for great listening and empowered her as a teacher of 40 exuberant five-year-olds in a time when there were no classroom assistants, few books and fewer pencils. Her pupils adored her!

I was about 6 years old in 1943, when she went to

take charge of a London County Council orphanage evacuated to Dawlish in South Devon. A large country house, The Cliffs was set in extensive grounds and had a secret tunnel leading to a smugglers' cove which was otherwise totally inaccessible except by boat. I was more than happy to spend time there, soaking up the adventures, sharing and caring with dozens of others my age, listening and learning within the safety of discipline, freedom and fresh air, whilst secretly pretending that I had been abandoned by my mother and rescued from oblivion. Just bliss!

Over the years she celebrated my joyous family life and guided and supported me through trials and tribulations of every kind with genuine deep concern and absolute commitment, then once retired, she bought a house in Carbis Bay, perched up high on the cliffs and another magical place to stay. She lived with her eccentric friend Crampy. I have no idea if they were a couple and no interest in the matter. In those days being gay was illegal, little understood and certainly not discussed or acknowledged. All I know is there were great parties with a variety of fun and games, singing and dancing, competitions and quizzes, and everyone was happy and fulfilled.

Aunty Phyl was an enthusiastic hiker and when age and infirmity overtook her, I was often despatched alone, complete with sketch pad and notebook to walk the walks she had so much enjoyed. This was long before digital cameras, mobiles and iPads, so it was a case of, once back at her house, talking her through what I had seen and she, with her acute mind's eye, would relive her wanderings in detail and was satisfied, thankful for the memory.

Gardening was an important part of her life and, although, however hard I tried, I have never managed to replicate the drifts of snow drops, and magnificent magnolias, cyclamen and camellias she grew in abundance, I do have an Escallonia bush grown from a cutting from her garden, that I cherish! She loved the promise of spring so daffodils always remind me of her love of life, great knowledge, patience and skills and we always celebrated Easter with due reverence.

She was once visiting my mother-in-law, both well in to their eighties with limited mobility but eager brains, when they announced an interest in pornography as they had absolutely no idea what it involved!! The top shelf of the local newsagent obliged and we left them with a magazine. After due diligence and scrutiny, they were satisfied that, though they were thankful for the information, the subject was not one they need spend time on and would we please carefully dispose of the evidence.

As Alfred, Lord Tennyson wrote, *Knowledge comes, but wisdom lingers!* Amen to that!

Fond Farewell

My much loved and respected Godmother was a venerable 90 when she died. She had been there all my life from the war years when I was very small, though my troubled teens to a wonderful wedding, subsequent motherhood, devastating divorce and beyond ... always there with words of wisdom and love. For many years she had tutored me in her funeral arrangements down to the finest detail about hymns, readings, who should play the organ and do the undertaking ... and, of course, the party afterwards.

Only when the time came did I realise that we had both overlooked one very important issue – what do with her remains. There was no objection to me taking her to a favourite hill top but a few raised eyebrows at my suggestion that she might like to be thrown off Lands' End!

I chose the time carefully to avoid the crowds and was somewhat taken aback when instead of being delivered in a small box, she actually filled a large sweetie jar. Nothing daunted, I set off up the hill humming happily, scattering her along the way. The path was narrow and winding so when a lady with a child and dog appeared, there was no hiding place. We smiled and greeted each other and she asked me what I was collecting ... when I explained, she asked if she might go with me and, together, we continued on our way (what happened to her companions I have no idea).   The final panoramic view was stunning from pitch-black clouds over the moors to hazy sunshine shimmering on the open sea and in between the verdant pastures of small hamlets and homsteads.   Birds, bees and a gentle breeze were appropriate accompaniments.

We prayed and, when I eventually opened my eyes, I was alone … the lady a small dot in the distance. Surely an angel in disguise!   For me that was a perfect ending and a wonderful new beginning. Thank you, Lord.

Respect and Understanding

For the thirteenth time, we moved house, exchanging the colourful and noisy life of a busy crossroads in Brixton for a quiet *cul de sac* in a leafy suburb of Birmingham.   Used to change, we soon settled in. Everyone spoke English and being within a stone's throw of the parish Church was an added bonus.

Next door lived a cheerful, elderly gentleman who kept himself to himself as he scuttled daily up and down the street with bulging plastic bags, stopping only briefly to pass the time of day.   It was a while before I learnt that he was the full-time carer for his housebound mother and never left the house for long.   I tried hard to imagine what it must be like to be so tied and still smiling.   One morning, I suggested that I could help out if he would like a break sometime. He beamed and disappeared, mumbling grateful thanks. Imagine my surprise when a few days later he knocked on my door saying my offer was an answer to his prayers and he had booked to go abroad for six weeks – I had envisaged a day or three at most! However, he insisted on paying most generously and, as I had no work at the time, extra income was welcome and I felt this was an answer to my prayers too.

Mrs Jones moved in to what we lovingly called the upstairs ballroom – large and airy, with tired décor but a fabulous view down our enormous garden. She was a most elegant, sophisticated and proud 97 years old, trapped in a body that prevented independence, and was understandably not best pleased at being suddenly relocated with strangers, albeit only next door. Before her son's taxi was out of sight, she started banging the floor and calling for attention. By evening of day one I was frazzled, but thankfully, after supper she was tired, ready for bed and settled.

In the morning, I quietly put her walking stick to one side and gave her a little bell which she rang incessantly but which was less irksome to my ears. Each meal was met with disdain and a curt "What's that?" which I found hurtful as I tried hard to cook appetising food that looked attractive. I was in despair, had no idea how to cope and was desperate for divine inspiration before disaster overtook us both.

First of all I asked why she was so disagreeable and demanding and her answer was a revelation. She felt lonely and afraid and needed constant reassurance. She got bored and often longed for stimulating company but only for short spells. Then I asked about her attitude to the food I made and she explained that it was hard to get excited unless she knew what was on the menu. She needed her taste buds tickled.

After that I made time each day to sit with her for a few minutes on a regular basis and always told her what I was cooking just before I served it. She was much happier and we soon settled into a routine with only minor hiccups. The indignity of being washed was anathema and she regularly accused the visiting nurse of being the district scrubber. I also made the mistake of putting broderie anglaise slips on the pillows which made her cross. She much preferred plain soft nylon ones that were kinder to her skin. When I asked what was the worst thing about being near 100 years old she said "Not wearing frilly knickers.". I bought some that fitted over her conti pads and we laughed. I learnt so much from her about life's experiences and remember her with love.

Hopefully, I have a better understanding about being geriatric that will stand me in good stead one day. [Next year is a big 0 birthday, but it's only a number – not old!]

At a time of great concern and the problems we all face in dealing with aging, may we remember those whose duty is to care in their own hoes or in residential places for the frail and elderly. We cannot ignore the fact neglect and abuse does exist and these difficult issues must be addressed sensitively and firmly. If you are worried, there is a Commission for Social Care Inspection [tel. 01452 632750] who will offer confidential advice.

Fine Food

Fish from the market, herbs dressed in oil,
Potatoes in the saucepan coming up to boil;
Fish in the frying pan, herbs tossed around,
Potatoes mashed with butter, salt and pepper ground.
Fish all crispy, brown and gold, herbs sparkly and green;
Potatoes soft and fluffy white all set out in a tureen;
A simple meal, a pretty plate, food prepared with care,
Fresh fish with herbs and tasty spuds:
A feast beyond compare!

The Perils of Parish Visiting

It has to be said... the Good Lord has a wicked sense of humour. Just as I think that I've got things right and am in line for a fair amount of praise, He sees things differently.

Each Sunday for a few weeks, on the way home from Church I called on a dear old lady confined to her house following a fall. She has always lived in Dursley and as a recent resident I loved hearing about the old days and went home feeling richer for the experience. This particular week was no different as she told me about the Victoria Cinema and graphic details of black and white films with the legendary stars who graced the screens. She made it sound so real and romantic. As we got to know each other a little bit; she trusted me to "Make I a cuppa afore ee goes"... so when she added, "and me bed is all of an 'eap on the floor an' I can't do it", I was happy to oblige.

The only other significant member of the household was a spoilt aristocratic marmalade cat, completely dominant as only feline friends can be. He, sadly, was not intelligent enough to distinguish between a commode in the kitchen and an outside convenience, or closed doors and a cat flap. It was as I gathered up the last of the bedding and stepped in a squidgy mess on the mat that I realised he had carefully covered up his turds as well brought-up cats do! If the mistress no longer trod the garden path to the lavatory, then why should he?

So, there was I - brought down to earth with a bump! Scrubbing and cleaning in my Sunday best. No longer the Lady Bountiful. just an ordinary neighbour.

How are the mighty fallen!

The Voice

I wanted to know the way ahead –
Each step marked out, unshaded by doubt
Flooded with light
And bright.
A path of ease
To please.

Then I saw him

His face was scarred
Hands marred.

In fear I signed
I cried "let me be"
But the voice said "follow me".

Something New

I did not hesitate when my neighbours asked me to feed their chickens whilst they were on holiday. Although I have never kept them, I have fond childhood memories of being with my beloved Granny (her of the wobbly bosoms, elastic arms, whiskery chin, infectious laugh and sparking eyes) in her small urban garden that boasted everything a larger rural plot might offer.

This time round, seventy year later, a lot of things seem to have changed. My temporary charges number only three, but it feels like thirty-three as they gather around my feet, excitedly exploring what this novice keeper might inadvertently allow. For starts, they are free range but with a designated, secure boundary fence to keep them off the flower garden. Sadly, the entrance gate is rather poorly and hanging off its hinges which makes it a tad difficult for a less agile human being to get in and out quickly. Fortunately, the rattle of a handful of corn in a plastic box persuades them to abandon the playground antics in favour of the feeding station in their run and we quickly established a pecking order.

They are big, friendly, fluffy brown jobs and I am so excited that they obligingly lay their eggs in the egg box, albeit in the company of huge, fragrant turds. I am quite sure that my Granny's flock were toilet trained as I never remember having to clean them out and NEVER came home covered in wood shavings with shoes caked in poo. These modern ones have a strict routine. Let out at dawn for a whole day of uninterrupted rooting and foraging, then a yummy mixture of nourishment delivered by me at tea-time, leaving time to digest it before another call for final lock-in but not before darkness has fallen and they have chosen to go to roost. Because I cannot see at night, I have an enormous torch to manage as well as the multiple security, anti-fox system and the new-laid eggs. If we had a neighbourhood watch they might alert NASA to the possibility of an alien landing! As it is, I am having fun enjoying the new experience and hoping that my neighbours will ask me to do it again. You are never too old to have a go at something new.

The Sound of Music

She was Mrs Williams, with her jet-black hair cut in an iconic Mary Quant style long before Mary Quant was an icon. We were a large class of stroppy fourteen-year-old school girls, much more eager to escape and run riot than to sit sedately in her music lessons, but she had us hooked each time, as she sat quietly and waited patiently for us 'to settle down'. All we could see was her head and shoulders and dainty black patent leather shoes, because her hands and body were completely hidden behind the raised lid and gleaming façade of the huge, elegant black grand piano which, as if by magic, produced the most amazing sounds. We were always soon silenced as our crazy, chaotic world shrank and we were lost in awe and wonder wanting more.

It was a puzzle how she managed to tame this raucous mob without raising her voice and resorting to meaningless sanctions which so many other teachers did, and well over six decades later, I remember her vividly and still ponder on the influence she must have had on countless pupils during her career. Her attention to detail and conviction that each one of us was worthy of encouragement, was infectious. Those with obvious musical talent, somebody with no interest or who was bereft of ability of any kind, were all treated equally and we knew that if the class was to escape the burden of order marks and extra homework, each one of us had an important part to play in the scheme of things. The idea of life skills and teamwork as a subject had not been invented so we were unaware of the value of the knowledge we were gaining as we diligently looked at lines punctuated with blobs, some black, some not, plus dots and tails and squiggly bits.

With a lot of repetitive practice, we found we were able to translate this jumble into a language of great satisfaction and joy and even dared to call ourselves singers although it took a long while to be recognised as a choir. We were disciplined, anxious to please and eager to learn. Our revered teacher never gave praise and only occasionally showed disappointment, but always by her example and expectations made us feel we could do better. Nothing seemed impossible as long as we worked together and had similar objectives. And so it proved as time went by.

In retrospect, I can see clearly how individually we can make a lot of noise which may be tiresome, irritating and non-productive, but together in harmony, with guidance and respect, even disparate groups of many minds, providing there is a corporate focus and inspiring leadership, can bridge gaps, foster ambition, develop hidden talents and achieve anything, any time and anywhere.

Altogether now – one, two three …

The Game of Life

My friend's brother died following a very brief but devastating illness. He was a confirmed bachelor, well beyond his allotted span of three score years and ten, a gentle galloping giant, still living alone in the family home, with three Siamese cats and umpteen TV sets. Amongst a number of hobbies, his favourite was cricket and his summers were devoted to supporting his beloved Somerset, along with a large group of like-minded friends. Otherwise, he quietly contented himself with a variety of D.I.Y projects, stubbornly refusing to relinquish his independence whilst keeping in touch by phone and very occasional visits to his only sister.

Perhaps he ignored the ravages of time and progressive illness, or maybe it happened suddenly, but when he presented himself at the GP surgery for the first time in thirty years, the receptionist had to delve deeply in the archives of medical records to find that he was actually on their register and still alive! Nothing much changed and he resumed his stubborn, solo survival strategy only admitting defeat when he was too weak to feed his cherished cats. Recognising the situation was serious, my friend and her daughter made the 200 mile dash to help, arriving shortly before he collapsed and was rushed to hospital, the centre of attention by paramedics in a drama of sirens and flashing lights in a normally quiet suburban neighbourhood where nothing of interest ever happened! We never discovered his reaction to such a commotion focused solely on him but hope he was reassured to know that he was safe in good hands, surrounded by love.

The next few days were spent in the spotless surroundings of a busy acute NHS hospital with comforting, caring nurses, medical and other staff, doing their very best for their patient and his family. It soon became clear that his prognosis was poor and the future would depend on a plan of care totally dependent on others for his every need! Tony had made it clear, he wanted none of that! Everyone closely involved respected his wishes and he died, with dignity and in perfect peace on a beautiful sunny day as the Somerset cricket team lost the battle in a hard-fought game! For him, too, it was the end of play.

We have nothing to fear in death, and everything to gain by making our wishes plain and desires known, which allows us to live to the end and our loved ones the certain knowledge they are doing what we want! I have had my coffin in my bedroom for several years, beautifully upholstered in white wool and in use as a blanket box, which I dare the moths to munch! In the beginning I did promise my daughters I would not use it as a spare bed! I have arranged my funeral service and also chosen my burial plot in a peaceful village country churchyard where I will join a number of my ancestors. My will is simple and reviewed from time to time!

Now, life in the slow lane just gets better, though horizons come closer and my travelling days are over. I see things more clearly in my mind's eye and am thankful for the life I have had and each new day that dawns.   I am no longer afraid of technology but use it with care especially to keep in touch with my Australian daughter and to play word games with friends who are too far away to visit. I do, reluctantly, ask for help and readily accept offers of assistance!

I am 81 years old and know that eventually "the Lord will rescue me and take me into His heavenly Kingdom." (Timothy 2 Ch4 v 18). I will be ready for lift off, but meantime there are games to be won, jobs to be done and people to see! To Him be the glory, for ever and ever. Amen

Biography of a Contented Man

He was a road sweeper in Dartmouth who spent his life clearing up litter, carelessly dropped by passersby. This man was totally devoted to his duty and lived, with his wife, on the river bank in a tiny cottage where I spent many happy holidays. There was no garage for he had no car! From the chimney oozed a tiny ribbon of smoke which hung on the air just long enough to scatter the scent of wood smoke before evaporating into the atmosphere.

No T.V. aerial cluttered the view. No T.V. The little windows boasted ice white curtains and in summer the sills were hidden by masses of blooms overflowing from window boxes. The front path wound through a maze of colourful shrubs and flowers to the gate which proudly announced "Rose Cottage" At the side, in the vegetable patch, grew an abundance of crops and the greenhouse was forever bursting with plants and seedlings all raised and tended by this loving man.

A cockerel strutted boastfully in a quarter of the plot set aside for him and his retinue of hens. For breakfast each day there was a new laid egg, with white so fluffy and yellow so big that it was almost a meal in itself before you tucked into toast made with home baked bread and marmalade. At the water's edge, a small boat was moored and when time and tide permitted and mackerel were about, a short trip, complete with fishing tackle, round the corner to the open sea, produced supper for a song.

Sunday was set aside as special, starting with morning prayer at the tiny church perched perilously on the headland, where countless generations over hundreds of years have worshipped and are laid to rest - if indeed the howling wind and crashing waves ever ceased long enough to give them peace. After lunch, he had 40 winks and then whatever the weather we would go walking. Up the hill, down the valley, along the beach or over the fields. His enthusiasm for our wonderful world was infectious as he taught us to respect and understand the treasures of our natural resources; consideration for others, the acceptance of some inevitable change but the courage to stand firm in the face of adversity. Above all to pray, thank God and trust in Him!

What joy to have known this wonderful man. He probably never considered he was a disciple, but that is how I remember him and I give thanks for his gentle teaching and wonderful example of how a simple life can be so fulfilling!

MY EPITAPH.
Let it be said by anyone who treads this way
That those she met, travelling day by day,
Only remember over many years,
Lots of fun, just occasionally dotted by tears!

The Golden Years

We first met when we were 16 years old, with birth dates a few weeks apart and began work at the Central Health Clinic in Tower Hill, Bristol. Our subsequent careers in different specialities, but both nursing, and family lives have run almost parallel. Though geographically for the most part distant, we have had a few years in middle age, as near neighbours which gave us the best of all worlds. By chance when we retired, we found two properties in a small country town, in an area new to both of us, opposite each other in a quiet back street, convenient to all amenities.

Together we rescued mine which had been lovingly neglected for a very long time. It positively beamed at being restored to its original 1914 state, and the dear little garden responded to essential care and was happy to be left to its seasonal happenings. As a traveller, I could pack up and leave it all for weeks at a time knowing it was not fretting.

Hers was a bigger house and an absolutely huge garden which she loved and in which she spent most of her time all year round. Together, when I was home, we daily walked her dog over the hills and far away before digging and hoeing, mulching and mowing for many happy hours at a time. Eventually for family reasons, she moved away and we began a new routine of visits for feast days when I would happily pack my little car for the relatively short hop up the motorway, which was a welcome change from global galloping to catch up with my three, adult offspring scattered round the world.

Now, suddenly it seems we have reached another significant milestone together, our 80th birthdays. Still teenagers at heart, we are solo survivors and age has not wearied us though our frames are more substantial, vision less than perfect (distance unaided most challenging) and hard of hearing desperately tiresome, to say nothing of incidental inconveniences that come with the passing years!

I am staying for a few weeks in her country home in Shropshire and our daily routine is simply stimulating: first thing in the morning she gets up, clatters about and eventually knocks on my bedroom door to deliver a welcome cup of tea, a treat I miss when I am at home alone. Next, she disappears with the dog, Tilly, very white and a small husky lookalike, to make a tour of the village and surrounds, meeting other early birds and collecting important information. There is no hiding place for anybody but a total absence of gratuitous gossip, which is genuinely refreshing.

Whilst they are out and about, I have my breakfast and scan the daily paper that always arrives around 7am courtesy of a little lad, not on a bike or by foot, but accompanied by Granny and her car. By 10.30 am we are ready to meet for coffee and implement the plans for the day that were laid out the night before. Shopping, sewing and knitting, cooking, occasional housework or sitting quietly with separate crosswords occupies us until lunch. Then it's my turn to go walkabout, accompanied by my faithful and sturdy mechanical machine which has four wheels and a seat but no engine. I can go for ever on person power though it takes time to go anywhere that is not flat and even. Sometimes to the farm to commune with the sheep, all individual shapes and sizes grazing the huge field with a distant backdrop of the Welsh Hills. Dozens of birds of all breeds and colours dart about low down or soar high above on thermals, all making their own way in the world.

If I take a different direction, I climb to the top of the hill and eventually reach the church, perched proud and high, built of deep red brick and looking comfortably welcoming like an aged and much-loved ancient in a cozy chair, pleased to see you and not going anywhere any time soon. Through the rather rough, but clearly cared for, churchyard there is evidence of recent burials alongside neglected areas of graves with obliterated writing and tilted headstones. I sit and ponder on lives and loved ones long gone and, in the distance spy the puff of smoke from the steam train as it plies its trade on the Severn Valley Railway line, tooting happily at level crossings, people and other hazards on the way.

I am immediately reminded of my childhood scenes and sounds, then teenage commuting by steam train and, much later, walks with my little boy near the crumbling country cottage we rented, when each day we stood on the bridge in the lane and waved to the engine driver. One memorable day he stopped and my son, aged about three and a bit, had a ride on the footplate.   Back in the real world, the church clock strikes four and everything stops for tea.

Magic Moments

"You know, my dear, if I were twenty years younger, I would take you on full time!"   Those words wrapped warmly round me like a duvet on a cold winter's night. He was so good-looking, over six feet tall, debonair, funny, widely travelled, drove a vintage car - low slung and sporty – and apart from the silver hair, could have so easily stepped out of one of those black and white films starring alongside Richard Todd or John Mills.

We met when I went to stay with an elderly lady in a picturesque North Cotswold village whilst her regular carer went on holiday.   This handsome stranger lived across the green in a pretty cottage with roses round the door by the mill race that gurgled happily on its way to join the River Windrush.

My free time was strictly limited to an hour in the afternoon when the old lady had a nap and late evening when she was comfortably tucked up in bed and, although quite safe on her own, I was by that time too tired to go far.

An invitation to coffee just over the way was a perfect solution. His music centre was extraordinary and collection of CDs vast. Despite his best endeavours I was never converted to his very favourite composter, Mahler, but he allowed me to indulge in never-ending renditions of all the classics and I couldn't have been happier in the best seats in any concert hall.

His tales of derring-do in the Second World War were compelling and it mattered not a jot to me that they have been embellished for maximum impact; it was like being with the real Guy Gibson.

Ours was a special friendship and over the following few years we kept in contact, mostly by letter and I looked forward to seeing him. When the old lady became frail and needed extra help, he was there as my refuge. Sadly, my visits came to an end all too soon. She died, I came home and never saw him again. He was eighty-four years old and I was sixty. Life moves on. The magic moments stay for ever.

Saving my Bacon

One of the many dictionary definitions of *dignity* is "of grave importance" and I am reminded of an event I once attended: full of reverence and fear, praise and thanksgiving, celebration tempered by tears of joy and, there too, in vain glory, was Pomp and Circumstance, Britannia's sister.

Huge in bulk, she would have been a perfect match for Goliath. Her bosom, amply decorated by bling, preceded her by a yard and nothing disguised the fact that she did not need cushions to make sitting on a wooden seat quite comfortable. Despite all that, she still felt the need to draw attention to her person and perceived status in society by turning to me and enquiring, in a loud voice "Don't you know who I am?".

From somewhere I conjured a polite rejoinder that, momentarily, satisfied and silenced her, albeit with the suggestion of a small smile. Nearby was a pole with a spikey thing on top that I longed to use to prick her ego and ease my discomfort at her demeanour. Mercifully, at that moment of temptation, I was distracted by a gentle face, atop a sober clad body, quietly advancing proceedings with what could only be classed as true dignity, demanding immediate and undivided attention to more important matters. Undoubtedly, the answer to a silent prayer from someone, somewhere.

Thank God for his omnipresence which stood me in good stead that day and often saves my bacon!

Darkness

The quietest tick from the smallest clock piercing the scary silent night as sharp as a samurai sword slicing through the sheerest silk is simply a sound you cannot see.

The thump of a heartbeat echoing like the blow from a blacksmith's mighty hammer hitting molten metal on the red-hot anvil by the fiery furnace, is actually keeping you alive. The gentlest breeze that could so easily cool the fevered brow must surely be the breath of the biggest dragon, determined to destroy everything in its path with one puny puff. Stifling darkness steals our breath.

Scary darkness is also the fiercest defender of the smallest creature, quivering in safe shelter and blinded by panic. Darkness is Nature's earthly winter womb nurturing Spring's beautiful, bountiful bloomers. It is blissful sleep, release from the pain of humiliating torture, debilitating illness and relentless ageing. The mystical place from whence we came. The ethereal eternity to which, one day, we will return to rest in peace.

Just pause for a moment and ponder. Slow down and reflect. Inwardly digest and start to move on, assured that darkness can be tamed and is a selfless ally in a frantic world. A gentle keeper and all-time friend.

Trouble in Paradise

Adam and Eve in the garden of Eden
Had plenty of time to spare.
They modestly dressed in fig leaves.
They had no clothes to wear.
Adam and Eve in the garden of Eden
Had oodles of time to spare.
They pleased themselves in Paradise,
'cos nobody else was there.

Adam and Eve in the garden of Eden
Had too much time to spare.
They foolishly ate the forbidden fruit
When the snake cajoled them to dare.
Adam and Eve in the garden of Eden
Have plenty of lessons to share.
They disobeyed God and were punished.
Hell's wrath came down on them there.

We can dream of the garden of Eden,
Convinced we'd make Paradise fair
So let's stay in that bubble
Keep out of trouble
And prove to God that we listen and care

There is Something for Everyone

A bit like an unplanned pregnancy, the idea was spawned from a chance encounter and a comment that landed in the attics of my brain early in 2011 and refused to be dislodged. A few short months later, Gertrude the Gardener emerged, already life-size, mature with a wisdom borne of the experience of years spent listening and learning form anyone she met. Made from bits and pieces found lurking in my 'busy cupboard', she is not very robust, but soon found comfortable sheltered accommodation in the large window of an empty shop in Parsonage Street, Dursley. She happily contributed to the efforts of the many, many people whose tireless efforts helped the town to a Silver Award in the "Britain in Bloom" competition in July, after which she went on a well-earned holiday.

Her fertile mind was not idle as she spent time at a secret destination where the sand is soft, the donkeys drive and the sea has always just gone out or is just coming in. Now back in her window apartment for all to see, she is bursting with ideas and enthusiasm for our 'Blooming Community' project and wants one and all to be included from the noughties to the nineties and beyond. There is endless space under her big umbrella for cherished dreams to be aired and, with the benefit of teamwork, maybe even grow to fruition. For the people – by the people.

It is not only about plants and people. It is about making our town the best we can by caring and sharing together; making do and mending, shopping locally and saving our High Street; eating well and exercising; beating the litter bugs and dog poo people; seeing problems as challenges that can become changes; spears becoming ploughshares and all organisations having one goal – a happy, healthy place that is the envy of England.

Gertrude says we do not need vast amounts of funds to make a start. A journey of a thousand miles begins with that first step and we know that great oaks from little acorns grow. Do-ers can be doing; be-ers can be beside them; pray-ers are essential too, in offering unseen support.

Each month has a theme so November is about preparation for hibernation and keeping warm. Draught-proofing and unearthing winter woollies. Planting bulbs indoors for Christmas and outdoors for Spring. Feeding the birds and finding glory in the grey skies, comfort in the dark nights safe at home with curtains drawn and a simple soup made from scraps. Learning from yesterday, using today and looking forward to the future with hope and expectation.

"We were yesterday's children, building castles in the sand, now we're building tomorrow, the future's in our hands."

Life after Childhood: For Neil, My Son

Set aside your web of worry,
gather in your thoughts and aims.
Stop the race, slow down the hurry.
Feed the fire, control the flames.
Freedom must be friend, not master,
Destiny is yours to mould
Time will go by faster, faster,
'til suddenly you wake up ... old.
Take this time and use it, share it,
Hold it, fold it, squeeze it, spare it,
Fetch it, catch it, watch it, patch it,
Make its shape, be brave and bold.
Every step you take is painful,
Frustration, boredom crowd you in,
People want you, need you, nag you,
Somehow you feel you cannot win.
Make a list of all you MUST do
And then what you most want inside,
Every day make little mountains,
Scale them quickly, log the ride.
Then one day you'll find your river,
First a trickle, then the tide.
Your loaded raft prepared and ready,
Uncertainty you set aside.
No-one knows what fate awaits you.
Everyday is hallowed ground.
The fun is seeing, minding, looking
Then using fully what you find.

This Global Village

I had to change planes at Kuala Lumpur, a busy little airport, totally devoid of brash sophistication, bold marketing or stress. Its modest website boasted a satellite tunnel which, in reality, reminded me of a Meccano set or one of those kindergarten drawings by a child excited at the prospect of covering a plain piece of white paper with random strokes from a fat black market pen. What at first looked like a primitive jumble of temporary scaffolding, was in fact a permanent structure immediately alongside shabby shacks that had an old-world charm. I loved it.

A loudhailer called us to board the flight to Sydney and my aisle seat, towards the back of the plane was one in a row of two. There was a steady stream of excited families and other travellers speaking numerous languages but the seat next to me stood stubbornly empty. Then, I noticed at the very end of the long line, a sad, rather plump, smart young man making his way slowly down the aisle, anxiously checking his ticket against the seat numbers until, with a look of great relief, he stopped by me and politely indicated that the vacancy was his allocated space. Soon after take off we fell into conversation, but he had such a soft voice and English, though perfectly pronounced, was clearly not his first language, so I had to listen very carefully to hear above the roar of the mighty jet engines. His story was both inspirational and sad. Full of hope and endeavour, liberally studded with doubt and uncertainty, care and concern.

Ten years ago, then aged 22, he had left his home in India to study engineering in Australia, leaving behind a close and loving family – Father, already a rich and successful businessman, Mother, four brothers, two sisters and umpteen other relatives. Once he had gained his university degree, he was offered a job in Sydney and happily stayed to further his chosen career. Meanwhile, back in India, a marriage had been arranged and he proudly showed me photos of his beautiful wife. She had willingly joined him to start a new life and they have been blessed with a son, now five years old, and are a happy household.

That could have been the end of the story. However, a few months ago, his mother became seriously ill and this young man did not hesitate to make plans to go to India, taking his wife and son with him. Mercifully, his mother is now well enough for him to feel able to leave her and go back to his job, but his wife and child are not eligible to re-enter Australia.

He is now between a rock and a precipice. Either to choose independence without his immediate family for the foreseeable future or the alternative in India, with every possibility of a financially successful career, surrounded by respected relatives but absolutely controlled by his father. After much heart searching, he has chosen the former, hoping that sooner, rather than later, the immigration authorities will see that he is a genuine hardworking person and will allow a permanent reunion. This was the first day of a long lonely journey. No wonder that he looked so sad.

When we landed, we parted company, having only exchanged given names and although he shyly said he hoped our paths might cross again someday, we both knew that that was not likely to happen, but I will always remember him.

The global village that is our modern and increasingly complex existence, offering so much choice and opportunity is also incredibly demanding, creating a tornado of emotions which need constant and careful attention, bearing in mind that the goal posts are always moving and we do not have finite resources. There is much to be said for the simple life bordered by a happy home and modest ambition, wherever in the world that might be.

George and Mabel

George was a handsome fellow. All muscle and big bones, his brow was broad and his huge skull housed a thinking brain, whilst dark brown wide set eyes missed nothing. He was as solid as a brick wall.

Mabel, on the other hand, was mean and lean. Her thin, pointed face and long sharp nose arrived long before the rest of her, as she suddenly and silently appeared from nowhere, alert and ready, acting with a mother's instinct to deter strangers and protect property and family. He might have been a night club bouncer or founding father and she the indomitable matriarch fronting a devoted clan, except that they were not humans, but handsome African hound dogs.

They had been my husband's faithful companions for many years as he pursued a career prospecting in the rich, alluvial diamond fields in Sierra Leone. A simple, nomadic existence, far from civilisation made quite comfortable by employing and paying a lot of local labour, especially a cook and water boy, and thoughtfully integrating into village life.

Each day from 5am. 'til dusk, about 5 pm, George would accompany the prospectors deep into the often impenetrable bush where constant danger lurked. Snakes and bitey things, poisonous vines and vegetation, uneven and marshy ground, rivers infested with tropical diseases to say nothing of hungry crocodiles happy to feed on humans. Probably most lethal of all, were the fierce tribesmen, often hidden in the trees, who were likely to shoot their venomous arrows first and then ask questions afterwards.

Mabel, meanwhile, stayed behind at the camp ready to defend it with her life if necessary. All this changed when I arrived as a young bride in 1961. My handsome husband standing 6 foot 4 inches tall was known, affectionately, as Big White Jumbo, so I was Big White Jumbo's missus. Then George and Mabel swapped roles. He stayed with me whilst she went off proudly to share each day with the work force. What prompted them, we will never know, but I was more than happy to have my very own bodyguard, totally loyal and absolutely invincible, to help me deal with any sort of unforeseen danger.

Jennifer with George and Mabel, Sierra Leone 1962

Uncertain Steps

We wandered alone in a strange land, not knowing
what lay ahead,
My family all felt quite shaken, so suddenly dragged,
unwilling from bed.
We wandered, it seemed, many hours alone, not
knowing what lay ahead,
Through desert, oasis and marshland, through
valleys deserted, barren and dead.
Much later, we came to a crossroads: THIS WAY and
THAT WAY signs read,
We pondered, alone in that moment, wondering
which way lay ahead.
THIS WAY well trodden, unhindered and straight,
the path showed no hindrance ahead;
Money galore, the telly and all! "Prosperity this way"
most said as THAT WAY was twisting and turned
out of sight, rocks barring the passage ahead, but
Far in the distance a star shone. "We should choose
THAT WAY" one person said!
We struggled along it for day after day, no progress
for miles ahead,
But, still, in the distance that star shone. "Will we
ever get there?" we all said.
Then, all of a sudden, a breakthrough occurred. "It
came to pass" a voice said:
"A babe has been born in a stable, the manger was
used for his bed".
Puzzled, we paused, unsure and afraid; uncertain of
what had been said.

"Follow that star" the voice came again. "Peace and Goodwill lie ahead".

Our faltering footsteps took us forward at first, but doubts hindered our progress ahead

As more popular tracks crossed our pathway. "Must we follow that star dead ahead?"

We did, and at last we arrived at the scene with the dazzling light overhead.

There were Joseph and Mary, so proud and sublime, baby Jesus safe-guarded by Ned!

Good Christian Men, rejoice, we heard: our nagging doubts soon fled.

Then prayers for peace, goodwill to all men as we knelt by the baby's head.

Next day, when I woke, the vision had gone, but excited I jumped out of bed

No longer wandering in darkness, wondering what lay ahead. So, now

Let's bow our heads and say our prayers, and think of those who tread

Life's weary ways and rugged roads, looking ahead with dread.

Let's show what Jesus means to us. His word we'll try to spread.

Dear God, help us to walk your way, each day that lies ahead.

Life

Summer Holidays

Rifling through some old recipe books, I was hurtled back to long summer holidays with picnics in the park as the huge Suffolk Punch horses patiently pulled grass cutting machines up and down and the smell of hay was intoxicating. The sun was always shining and we had so much fun for free. We only went home when the food and drink was finished or it started to get dark.

We ran about or sat and made daisy chains or squeaky sounds with blades of grass. We tormented the poor park keeper who sometimes told us off, but I honestly can't remember what upset him, except that we might have bypassed the hut where you paid to go on the tennis court, hopped over the fence and, briefly, pretended to be on the Wimbledon grass. We played with scruffy balls and old wooden bats, wearing play clothes and tatty daps which was not acceptable to the ruling class. Even austerity demanded that smart white outfits and proper gym shoes were the dress code on the hallowed ground!

Almost more exciting was to sneak on to the Bowling Green with its immaculate lawn, so tempting to a gang of eight-year-olds with endless energy and the ability to vanish without trace should any adult appear and threaten to report us. We had catapults crafted from elastic bands and bits of twig and used the porcelain separators on the telephone wires for target practise, but never near our homes just in case we broke any and got into bother.

There were huge conker trees to climb and little copses to play hide and seek in. Our energy was boundless and we were blessed to have nothing else to worry about! I am glad I was born so long ago when life was simple and days were long.

A Cautionary Tale

There was a naughty little mouse whose name was Tiny Tim,
With toffee he filled his Father's hat, right up to the very brim.
He hid his Mother's slippers and upset the baby's pram,
He was a naughty little mouse and ate his sister's jam.
He strayed away from home one night, he shouldn't have done that.
He isn't naughty any more, 'cos he's inside a cat!

I was nine years old when I wrote this poem and it was published in the Pillar Box column in the Bristol Evening Post.

First, Say Thank You

In the beginning, aged about five, I was an avid follower of Christopher Robin.

Hush, hush, whisper who dares.
Christopher Robin is saying his prayers

Then at my beloved Bristol Granny's knee (her of the wobbly bosom, twinkling eyes and whiskery chin), I learnt that when we ask, God always answers. Sometimes "yes" and sometimes "no" and sometimes He needs space and time to think things over. Then we must "bide our souls in patience and trust in His redeeming love" she said.

It was war time and with my limited experience of life, my petitions were simple but never the lest VERY important. Loppity, our pet rabbit, had worms and, I knew, felt poorly. I prayed. He got better! Human intervention had no place in my vocabulary. God had heard and answered: easy!

During frequent air raids we spent boring hours hunkered in an Anderson shelter, very often dark and damp, with little to do but sing songs and listen to stories while German planes droned overhead en route to the city and the docks. At the first sign of the "all clear" siren we would dash out and comb the garden for shrapnel, bits of burnt parachute and other treasures which made an exciting collection. That novelty eventually wore off so I suggested to the Almighty that it would be fun to have a little bomb drop nearby, just enough to make a big hole in the ground and blow a few windows out. Nothing too serious, but sufficient to relieve the monotony. A few days later He duly obliged just as I had imagined it, and I was hooked on the power of prayer.

I did have a problem when the baby my mother was supposed to be producing did not materialise. Hushed grown-up voices and false smiles were confusing and God seemed to have gone on holiday. One day, somebody explained that my little sister would not be coming home as she had died. I knew about Jairus' daughter, so was quite sure that Hilary would be raised and when, despite waiting patiently, it didn't happen, I felt let down. On reflection, it is interesting that my six-year-old self apparently accepted the situation and was soon back to being Granny's "varmint", no doubt expecting things to go my way once more. I needed more patience!

Looking back over a troubled and volatile youth, I realise prayer did not feature greatly in my day to day existence but that I was never far from faith. During many years as a nurse, I often dedicated my patients in silent prayer and, much later as a mother, I constantly pleaded that my young tearaways would survive their various extreme sports and expeditions. I took it for granted that it was as easy as that. God automatically takes care of things.

About twenty years ago, a chance comment changed my attitude. My friend had been summoned to her sick parents and I was to go with her. To my surprise, as we loaded the car and *before* we set off on the long drive, she gave thanks for our safe arrival. That was puzzling to me, but what a revelation that, as the weather deteriorated and traffic increased, we were totally relaxed and not at all weary at journey's end. Since then, I try to remember when the going gets tough, to give God the glory first, with grateful thanks for the solutions as yet unknown.

This week, I set aside a day to concentrate on a challenging needlework project, despite the fact that I can write "I love you" in the dust around house. I had been sewing for a while when my needle inexplicably vanished without trace. Not good news! I politely thanked God for finding it and carefully looked but nothing happened. Reluctantly, I crawled around on all fours, cleaning every inch of carpet, moved and dusted the furniture and scrutinised the contents of the Hoover before finally giving up and retiring, dismally, to the kitchen to put the kettle on. There, like a beacon of bright light on the worktop was my needle. No more time that day for sewing as planned, but I had done some long overdue spring cleaning.

God is working his purpose out, as year succeeds to year and I am extremely happy about that, but it may be some time before I am persuaded to make housework a priority!

2011

The Rain Forest

Some trees stand slender, straight and true
Stretching, reaching way up into the sea of blue.
Underneath the shadowy, sun-draped shade
Bush turkeys strut and scratch the scrunchy leaves.

Suddenly a flash of brown and white
A kookaburra sweeps down to claim his tasty prize:
The newt-sized lizard lazing in the sun
No match for silent flight and telescopic eyes.
Butterflies hop by on brilliant wings and
Spiders spin their webs of tensile strings
Somewhere beyond the shadowy, sun-draped shade
Bushwhackers make noise with big boys' toys.

Suddenly a flash of green and red
A parrot swoops down to feed on seeds
Set out in shelter from the scorching sun,
No match for hunting in the humid heat
Easier to eat and so much tastier than weeds.

My Best Friend

I really have no idea how, why or when it all started, but perhaps A.A. Milne could claim at least some credit. As a very young child, I remember kneeling at the foot of my bed, warmly wrapped in a fluffy pink dressing gown, which had been lovingly created by my thrifty mother from something that had had a previous life elsewhere. (During the war bags of 'pass-ons' regularly did the rounds and reappeared transformed to new use!)

Hush, hush, whisper who dares.
Christopher Robin is saying his prayers

I was totally mesmerised and avidly listened to the silence, often in flickering candlelight or the dim beam from a fading torch battery, effortlessly blocking out all distractions such as muffled adult conversation and distant explosions. Despite the prolonged absence of my mother, due to illness, and my father on active service, I was always secure in the knowledge that I was loved way beyond my earthly nurture that, despite austerity, was more than adequate. Jesus was my best friend.

It never occurred to me to share this with other people or that it was anything other than quite normal. He and I had private conversations which, in my small world, mattered only to us but were still mightily important and needed quiet time for serious discussion. There was great comfort in emptying my mind of niggling worries – great big important words like *anxious* that grown-ups said a lot but that I could not spell and did not understand: multiplication tables beyond 8 seemed totally incomprehensible and Loppity, our long-haired rabbit, had worms.

As time went on, I saw less need to confine my time with Jesus to night-time prayers and used to reel Him in whenever I needed to chat. Unlike adults who were often involved in other matters or did not appear to understand (how was I supposed to know that they cared too but were struggling with a threatened imminent invasion by Germany?) Jesus was consistent, calm and consoling.

He was gentle in his reprimands about my misdemeanours and a comfort to an increasingly active, adventurous and curious child like me. Even when I was made reserve instead of being in the 1st XI school hockey team, He seemed to be OK about that and encouraged me to keep trying despite the disappointment.

Years later, as a wife and mother juggling a career and busy family life, I was often overwhelmed by apparently impossible hurdles and situations. My three teenage children used to tease me gently as I disappeared for what they called "God business" and were happy knowing that an hour later, I would be back with a clear head and able to sort out everything (well, almost everything!).

Now, in my seventies, and thankfully enjoying extra time in this game called life, I am still excited by the parent/child relationship I have with Jesus and that we continue to journey together just the same. I am glad to be old and retired and content to be bobbing along on the bottom with ears and eyes that work a treat, aware that my lips sometimes need a zip and so grateful for two replacement hip joints. Each day begins and ends with Thanksgiving; a site meeting with the Master to mull things over and share concerns in peace without distractions. If only we could all manage a few minutes of regular quiet contemplation, what a difference it would make. Jesus could be your best friend too.

2010

Sydney Side

Just beyond the rooftops the ocean's peeping through
The waves a rash of white spots, pinpoints in shades of blue
Hazy, crazy cotton clouds make patterns in the sky
A constant hum as cars in crowds relentlessly drive by
Just beyond the rooftops the ocean's peeping through
A dozen all-sized sea yachts pinpoints in shades of blue.
Hazy crazy cotton trails make patterns in the sky
A constant hum as planes and things relentlessly fly by.
Just beyond the rooftops the oceans peeping through.
It ebbs and flows and never stops and stays forever blue.

Food for Thought

It was 1943, the middle of World War II and I was 6 years old. A confused child consumed by insecurity and angst despite being surrounded by an extended family including my brother, grandparents, aunt, uncle and cousins but no parents. Nothing made sense. I was angry and rebelled. I was rude and constantly rejected all attempts to persuade me to change.

"Could you just try being nice to people?" my brother pleaded one day.

I refused to listen. "No way!" was my instant retort and life went on the same. We spent hours in the air raid shelter as bombs dropped round about and I dreamt of being out there, fighting fires, helping casualties, being useful and free!! I did not understand.

Then one day I saw my father walking down the street, immaculate in his RAF uniform. He had been away so long and this was an unexpected 48 hours leave. Gently he told me about his role in the war and how my mother was desperately ill in hospital, which explained their absence. Suddenly everything fell into place. There was a distinct possibility that things would get more difficult and that we should all make an effort to help each other. That he may not be around but that he would always be with me. How important it was that we said our prayers and kept our faith whatever happened. Assurance crept over me. All was well in my world.

Later that day, he took me to a very smart restaurant in Bristol (Hort's which I believe was at the top of Park Street) as a treat. Mindful that money was very short I was careful to choose a cheap meal. It happened to be tripe and onions and a particular favourite of mine. Sawdust stew would have been just as good, for the most important fact was that I was alone in a crowd, with my beloved father, sharing a very special meal, which not only fed my body but my soul.

That treasured memory has stood me in good stead over the years, especially as family meal times can so often be superseded by fast food and snatched snacks on the run. It reminds me how blessed we are to have freedom to speak and food to share. Above all, each time I take Communion, I give thanks for that special earthly experience that makes sharing the bread and wine even more moving.

2003

How did it begin?

A reflection by Rev Ian Gardner during a recent Thursday morning Holy Communion Service at St. James set me thinking. It was a rhetorical question about how we first came to faith.

This is my story ... In 1943 I was six years old and one of a number of children of similar age living in neighbouring houses on a quiet road in Weston Super Mare. I felt sorry for the others whose fathers were always about and seemed weighed down and woebegone as they left their homes at exactly the same time each day and returned at tea time apparently exhausted and untidy! My Daddy, on the other hand, was permanently away and in my mind, winning the war, single handedly saving us all! My handsome hero, out of sight but not out of mind as his RAF unit responded to the threat that Hitler posed to the world!

One of our neighbours was a single lady, absolutely devoted to her role as a school ma'am as well as caring for her aged mother. Every Sunday, immediately after lunch, she gathered all us children together and we would catch the bus into town to the Wadham Street Baptist Church which was an amazing building of awe and majesty but warm and welcoming to a gang of excited small girls so used to austerity and bland surroundings.

We were her "little lambs" and we obediently responded to her quiet voice, confident in her gentle but firm herding skills, knowing we were safe with her and would never get lost. The minister was a mountain of a man, wearing floaty black clothes with his double chin resting comfortably on a crisp white neck tie below a big square mouth and large nose, and eyes popping out from behind enormous black-framed specs. His frame seemed to fill the building and his voice echoed from the marble pillars and bounced off the balcony with minimal effort on his part and greatest effect on his small crowd of eager listeners.

It was Sunday School and we were there to learn from the one available book, which was enormous and boasted beautiful paintings by Margaret Tarrant illustrating the most exciting stories gathered together in what we found out was The Bible. We loved the Old Testament tales of derring-do, goodies v baddies and satisfactory outcomes from unpromising scenarios but the New Testament for me was where it all came together.

JOY meant Jesus first, others next and yourself last which made sense when our daily lives were constantly interrupted by wailing sirens warning us of air raids, quickly followed by scuttling to the shelters, hearing bombs drop and hoping for the all clear! I felt sure of my safety as the seeds of Jesus's love were sown in my fertile brain. He was my Heavenly Father and permanent friend who comfortably joined my absent earthly father in providing me with total belief that whatever we faced, all would be well. Together, we had a focus.

Over the years I have never lost that first feeling of joy, peace and direction, together with a great appreciation of those who were there at the beginning, those I have met along the way and countless numbers who have shared my journey but are no longer part of it. I have no regrets (except that I never owned a longed-for life-sized wooden rocking horse) and am constantly reassured that through all the changing scenes of life, Jesus remains my constant companion and friend together with my loved ones who have died but will never be forgotten. Mine is a simple faith which endures and frees me from doubt and anxiety of the unknown whilst leaving room to hear other points of view.

I know where I'm going, just not when, so every day is the Lord's Day. There is much to do!

Try As We Might

It was wartime. The Church Minister was a BIG man with jet black hair and horn-rimmed specs to match. We were a mixed group of 6–9-year-olds gathered up by a kindly spinster and taken regularly on public transport to Sunday School. The Baptist Church was a wonderful place with balconies and marble pillars, fabulous stained-glass windows and a dome to rival St Paul's Cathedral. A veritable theatre where we acted out little hearts out. All the parables and stories Jesus told came to life and the joy was infectious.

Our beloved Pastor implored us to "lift the roof for Jesus" as we sang our favourite hymns and fervently praised the Lord. Somehow, it was never enough. We strived hard in all our endeavours, especially during the week when we still did our best, knowing that He was watching over us.

Then it happened!

We arrived at Sunday School as usual and found a big hole in the roof. We could see the blue, blue sky and Heaven – Success!

We were overcome with such excitement and expected the grown-ups to be pleased. As we scrambled through the rubble in the ruins we did not begin to understand the adult talk about bombs and Hitler. Whoever he was he had nothing to do with it and we deserved applause. Subsequently, Sunday School moved to a dusty upstairs hall with little light and low ceilings, but we still had huge fun, being Good Samaritans and shepherds, soothsayers and seed sowers. I am grateful for all that.

2000

String of Steel

I spy with my little eye, a spider;
I spy with my little eye, a fly beside her.
Unseen by my little eye, a string of steel;
Unseen by the little fly whose pain I feel.
She spins him in a silk cocoon
That shimmers like a silver spoon.
Then once she's sure he's safe in store,
She mends her net and waits for more.

The Tropical Storm

Great big blobs of crystal rain fall from the leaden
sky
Bouncing off the parched red earth after months of
scorching dry.
Gutters fill and overflow, puddles form and grow
and grow,
Rivers bowl and pitch and run, scoring points and
having fun.
Listen to the wind as it thunders through the trees,
Some it hammers, some it bashes, bringing others to
their knees.
Hear the quiet when it's finished, feel the stillness of
the storm,
See the beauty of the branches, every shape and
form.

Squandering the Bounty

My happy, wartime childhood was spent in a neat, semi-detached house on a quiet road. I was a lucky little girl with a bedroom of my own which, being larger than my brother's, I willingly vacated for the occasional visitor staying overnight. The views from my window were magical and full of promise to my infant eyes; a wonderful world just waiting to be explored! Over the hills and far away Africa, India and China beckoned impatiently. The adjacent park, I was sure, stretched to infinity and beyond although Buzz Lightyear was still waiting to be born.

I could see no restrictions even when I discovered there were limits, and places forbidden to children where, for example, old people played what looked like a boring game, rolling big brown balls up and down an immaculate lawn. In another part, a notice read DANGER KEEP OUT on a barbed wire fence surrounding the ruins of the boating lake recently wrecked by something called the blitz.

That needed closer examination and detailed investigation for clues to solving this mystery and we had exciting finds. Bits of shrapnel and burnt parachute were not uncommon. A spooky darkness prevailed in the glade where handsome horse chestnut trees stood tall, apparently touching the sky, boasting beautiful white candles in the springtime, followed by shiny, burnished conkers which provided hours of interest and fun. No health and safety interference and we survived it all.

I never minded when my mother confined me to my room to reflect on what I thought were minor misdemeanours that she saw as reckless hooliganism, because I sat in my window and pondered on the far distant hills, a reminder of strength, consistency and permanence when everything around me seemed in flux. It was my own Kilimanjaro, the very name conjuring up romantic notions and filling my head with dreams many of which, I am glad to say, came true in later life.

Seventy-five years on, it saddens me to see my grown-up grand-daughter's pain when she realizes that concrete covers the places where she and her young friends used to play when she stayed with me in the school holidays. On the other hand, she has just spent a year working her way round the world, equipped with little money, a rucksack and a Rough Guide, collecting information, first hand, about how heedlessly the precious and vulnerable bounty everywhere is being squandered. Such experience is influential, sowing seeds and scattering random thoughts for consideration, however improbable. Some, if only a few, will take root and make all the difference as she makes her individual way in our ever-changing and shrinking world.

Maybe each succeeding generation finds progress and development a double-edged sword, dangerous, difficult and disturbing, exciting and enduring. I am glad I am old and can sit in my window with a perfect view of Cam Peak in the distance, assured that some things remain constant. There are mountains that will never be moved but by the same token, the mighty sea is only powerful because of millions of little drops working, not always in unison, but always responsive and effective. Together we stand, divided we fall and despair is not an option.

The accompanying photo was taken recently by my son, a teacher in Bamaga, a remote area at the very tip of North Queensland. It only took him and his students a couple of hours to collect massive amounts of rubbish washed up and littering their beach at Cape York on Endeavour Strait. Paradise in danger of being lost. We may not be near the sea, but that is no excuse for doing nothing about the dangers our planet faces from drowning in plastic waste.

Rubbish recently washed up on the beach on Endeavour Strait in remote North Queensland

My First School

I have no idea why my introduction to full-time education was at an all boys school. It was war time and my father was in the RAF. I didn't talk to my mother a lot so never bothered to ask. What I do know is that I was not enamoured of the confines of domestic life or the expectation that all little girls played with dolls. I just loved the hurly burly of the playground and the freedom boys were allowed to be tough, take real risks and be bold. I loved the classroom with high windows that shut out the world, and in the middle stood a huge cast iron stove, like a dragon monster munching all manner of rubbish that burnt furiously and kept us warm.

Brian and Jennifer first school uniform

Best of all, I loved our teacher, Mrs Wall, who made learning interesting and fun, so England had a backbone called the Pennines, Norfolk had a wash and Tasmania, the Apple isle, sat like a pimple on Australia's chin. Every day my brother (who was 9 years old and my guardian) and I walked the three miles up over the hill, through the park and along the main road, happy to have purpose and structure in our little lives. Even challenges like being caught in the open in an air raid, or patching me up when I was run over by a car, added to our sense of invulnerability.

Then it all went horribly wrong!

There was a very smelly boy in the class who was being bullied. I was only five years old, but felt the sense of injustice and a compulsion to do something about it. So, without asking, I borrowed some clothes from home and next day took him in the school toilets to get him cleaned up. Sadly, the Head master did not ask for an explanation but sent me packing with a note that "she is rather a madam when let off the leash". I was not allowed back and subsequently went to a prissy girl's school to be taught how to be a lady. But that is another story!

We Don't Need Super Nannies

I was a Brownie in the 10th Weston-Super-Mare Pack and we met, weekly, in a spacious wooden hut on top of a grassy knoll. Our leader was tall and thin, sharp with a shapeless figure, steel rimmed spectacles and short straight hair. She never smiled and rarely gave praise. We were raw material needing to be shaped - she reminded me of a blacksmith putting rough iron in to a fiery furnace before moulding and hammering it in into shapes, useful, reliable, endurable and strong.

We were disciplined, but she never raised her voice in anger and we all promised to do our very best "to do our duty to God and the Queen, and to do a good turn every day". Others came first. There was a purpose and comfort in working as a team and helping each other to achieve our highest aims. *United we stand, divided we fall* was a maxim I came to appreciate much later in life.

First tests like Golden Bar and Golden Hand, were tailored to age and experience whilst badges which came later were earned by due diligence and application. Gradually our uniforms boasted decoration and earned respect from the initiated and spurred us on to greater things until our "wings" enabled us to fly up to Guides.

One of the many basic skills I learned and still use today, was how to organise the washing up without wasting huge amounts of water! Everything we did had meaning and purpose, from daily living at home to Thinking Day which was an annual event celebrating the movement worldwide. Brownie Revels brought local packs together to meet and share fun and games usually in the Summer although not always on a sunny day! We were involved in raising money and all sorts of events. I recall, particularly, visiting less fortunate children and families at Christmas in cold dark dreary houses. We learnt humility too.

My mother always made sure my uniform was immaculate (I even insisted she polished the insteps of my shoes!!) and I was the envy of everyone as I constantly won maximum points at our inspections. Then one day my bubble burst as Brown Owl asked me to hand her my brass badge, proudly pinned to my perfectly ironed tie. I did so eagerly, expecting that she would hold it up as a shining example of good practice. However, she turned it over and revealed the back which was covered in verdigris!!

There was a collective intake of breath and no hiding place for me. I was mortified and learnt a salutary lesson. I am so grateful. We don't need super nannies and government funding. Just more Brown Owls.

Fog

The shadows lurked on the corner
Then danced up the foggy wall
The silence closed in all around me
Nobody would answer my call

I turned my back on the shadow
Afraid and unwilling to move
The darkness threw arms all around me
I struggled, my courage to prove.

One step was very uncertain
Direction unsure and unwise.
The fog wound a web all around me
A voice said: "Here is my prize!"

Nobody was there – not a human,
There wasn't a person in sight.
The breeze did a dance all around me
And waltzed off in the fog and the night.

Left there alone and so lonely
Imagining pitfalls and ghosts
Doom and disaster around me
Ten gibbets on all the lampposts

The dew made a pattern – quite pretty –
But silence cannot be endured
My face touched the cobwebs all round me
My madness was all but assured.

I woke with a start the next morning
Afraid of what I should find,
But my eiderdown quilt was all round me
I was sound in all limbs and my mind.

The Holy Cross

The Holy Cross is a beginning which has no end
It just IS, everywhere we care to look
The cross is a focus without barriers
Of language, creed or culture.
In reality, one shape but any size
Any medium and anywhere
A target for today, a pause for thought
A meeting place that reaches all points of the compass
Out into infinity and beyond
A sanctuary of spiritual safety
A silent mentor or collective collaborator
Without it we run the risk of being poor
And weak and lonely
With it we can be rich and strong and together
A cross in your pocket is equal to a wallet full of money

It's the Stuff of Fairy Tales

In 1952 I was 15 years old and he was 17, tall and handsome, with impeccable manners and interesting conversation. He lived just down the road from us in Weston-super-Mare and we fell in love. Sadly, there was a snag. He and his family were one time refugees from the Raj and had brown skin. My parents disapproved and forbade us seeing each other.   Accidental meetings had to be carefully arranged (our old dog suddenly enjoyed extended walks!) until National Service took him away. I left home to start my nursing career and we lost touch.

Surprisingly, life went on and many years later, in Birmingham, my teenage daughter fell in love. No doubt, to her, he was Prince Charming and they were obviously happy together but I had a problem. He was black. Somehow I forgot (or chose to ignore) my own experience, refused to accept the situation or get to know him and squandered many months in heartache as their friendship flourished. Then my beautiful daughter fell gravely ill and had to have major life-saving surgery. I was devastated, alone and felt helpless. Everything spiralled out of control and nobody could help. I prayed.

As time went by in a blur, I began to realise that throughout it all, her young man had been steadfastly supporting both of us, unobtrusively taking care of all our needs. He was a tower of strength during her long recovery and although they later parted, he remains a family friend to whom I owe a great debt of gratitude. Through him, I learnt that people are gift-wrapped parcels – you have to get beyond the outer layers to discover what's inside.

What about my teenage sweetheart?   After 45 years we had a joyful reunion and still keep in touch. He is handsome, funny, tall and interesting and back living in his old home where for some time he looked after his mother until she died. We happily reminisce about our romance and what might have been, but have no regrets. Life would have been very different but not necessarily better and we have fun swapping stories and experiences. I feel so blessed and constantly thank God for "working his purpose out as day succeeds to day".

Friends are like angels who lift us to our feet when our wings have trouble remembering how to fly. Let us be thankful.   2005

Anything is Possible

I was a determined 6-year-old and had my life planned out. At the first opportunity I would take my place by the side of Albert Schweitzer in Lamberene. I knew that with his snow-white hair and long beard he was the nearest thing to God on earth, lived in Africa and looked after lepers, those sad outcasts of society. I wanted to be his helper.

My mother was not impressed by my ambition and insisted that my education was most important if I were to achieve anything. School was a great trial to me (a few years ago I met one of my old Grammar School teachers who confirmed that I was a frustration to her); I was bright, loved history, geography, English and sport but saw no point in studying when there was a whole wide world out there needing my attention. It might take time, but nothing would stop me going to Africa.

The moment I was 16, I stepped on the first rung of the nursing ladder and throughout my training surprised everyone by getting good grades without much devotion to books. Sadly, I never got to Lamberene, but I lived in the bush in Sierra Leone in 1962 and later visited Kenya. Then in 1989, at a particularly low point in my life, suddenly single, lost and lonely on a downward spiral of self-destruction (even God seemed to have gone on safari) I found myself on a plane heading for Malawi.

Certain that I had an immediate and permanent mission there, I packed up my life in the UK and set out in supreme confidence and self-importance. After several days travelling, I reached a very poor area in the south of the country where drought, disease and famine had a strong hold. My contact was Grace, a wonderful local African, 6 ft tall and built like a brick wall, but even she was struggling to survive. Things looked bleak, but I had arrived and would change all that. How arrogant!

There was so much to be done. As well as poverty, there were crippling political restrictions. Family planning was forbidden and overpopulation made matters worse. We walked for miles in searing heat to reach villages where queues of people waited patiently for medical advice and would give anything for medicines and dressings. Getting to Church often meant a two hour trek through the bush and latecomers were not only banned from the service, but also punished.

Despite their hardship, the people I met were amazingly cheerful, positive and resilient. I realised that if I stayed long I would become a liability, not only because my outspoken views displeased the politicians who would lose no time in putting me in prison, but also because there was so little food, I soon became physically weak.

Returning to England, I felt a failure but had reckoned without the Lord. First and very soon I felt free to talk about my experience and quickly raised money for a bicycle and trailer for Grace to do her rounds. Then a cow in calf which was the start of a dairy herd, followed by a hen coop and flock of chickens for eggs and food. One night, at a very posh dinner party in Birmingham, and much to my surprise, I pledged to build a meeting house in that same African village to be used as a Church, clinic, nursery and school. At the end of the evening a lovely lady gave me £10. That was the start of a long journey that took three years of fund raising by a lot of people of all ages from the noughties to the nineties, pounds and pennies raised in all sorts of ways from pram pushes by toddlers to marathons by pensioners, sponsored silences by teenagers and knit-ins by mothers to name but a few. It was a huge project supported by faith and trust and succeeded beyond our wildest dreams, bringing such joy and hope to many both here in England and over there.

Grace eventually died of an AIDS related illness, but I am glad to have known her and able to play a small part in helping her extended family. It just goes to show that nothing is impossible when we walk with the Lord. I could not have done it alone.

The Sea Beneath my Feet

It all began with a chance remark in 2007 while I was recovering from one hip operation and waiting for another. I had mentally retired my body from active service which allowed my brain time to take in all sorts of trivial information that could otherwise have gone unnoticed

As a little girl I loved any stories of daring-do, but top of my favourites ruled Grace Darling, closely followed by anything else to do with the sea and I willingly donated my pocket money to the Mission for Deep Sea Fishermen whenever there was a collection.

For two weeks each summer from 1946 when I was 9 years old, until my late teens we went to Teignmouth where I spent as much time as possible aboard the bright red m.v. "Restless" taking short trips around the bay,

Syd Hook and Jennifer 1950

days out trawling or just messing about afloat! Her skipper, a fisherman appropriately named Syd Hook, with his burnished skin and curly pipe was my real-life hero and I knew that, however rough the sea, as long as I obeyed his commands, I would be safe. In fact I believed that had I fallen overboard he would have saved me from getting wet! Such is faith!

 So, when I heard that the Trinity House Flagship "Patricia" (86 metres and 2451 tonnes) undertaking

maintenance of navigational buoys, refuelling offshore lighthouses and dealing with wrecks round the coasts of England, Wales and the Channel Islands, was also taking passengers, I wanted to be one of them. As soon as I had the date for my second op., I booked my passage, allowing five months to get fit and celebrate my 70th birthday... there is no age barrier but you must be able to scale a rope ladder in an emergency.

Departure day dawned and I was nervous but the moment I drove in to Swansea Docks and saw the ship I felt at home. There were nine passengers to thirty-two crew. The week was full of adventure, with every sort of weather from gales and lashing rain to thick fog to calm sea and visibility of 32 miles!

We were welcome on the bridge and saw at close quarters the great skill and huge responsibility of the Officers of the watch. Likewise, from another vantage point we were close to the sailors on the lower deck as they used their strength and team training to maintain safe channels in the busy shipping lanes of the Solent by checking and changing marker buoys. Below decks and unseen, were countless other hands, from cooks and carpenters to engineers and launderers, working tirelessly to ensure everything was shipshape and Bristol fashion. Because of the discipline, devotion to duty and team work of the whole ship's company together, we had total freedom in absolute security. Eyes and ears constantly tuned in case of need! How different from life on land!

By chance I learned from the Captain that m.v. "Restless" still plies her summer trade, still painted bright red, and that Syd Hook still lives in the same cottage on Ivy Lane, so I took courage and went to see for myself. He is 88, nearly blind and very frail but has lost none of his charm and is still mentally alert with an amazing memory. We easily bridged the gap of the missing years and found great comfort in talking about old times and family members we have loved and lost but who are still alive to us both. I also discovered that he was torpedoed serving in the Royal Navy during the war and since then has been involved in countless courageous rescues as a Lifeboatman, coastguard and sea pilot and has a cupboard full of medals to show for it. Truly a legend in his own lifetime and I feel so blessed to count him as a very dear friend and mentor who had such an influence on my growing up (second only to my Dad and granny) and is still alive so I can tell him how much he means to me.

I thank God for the opportunity to see him again even if addressing the physical ravages of time is painful and unsettling. It is worth it. At the going down of the sun, and in the morning, I think of him.

The Voice

I wanted to know the way ahead
Each step marked out
Unshaded by doubt
Flooded with light and bright
A path to please of ease
Then I saw Him
His face was scarred
Hands marred.
In fear
I sighed
I cried: "Let me be!"
But
The Voice of Love
Said: "Follow me"

Ghosts of Christmas Past

It is hard to believe that another year is drawing to a close, for the most part to disappear into unrecorded history, for however hard I try, keeping a diary becomes tedious and time-consuming and the novelty quickly wears off after a few weeks. I am left with a lot of blank pages, not a little regret and a resolution to try and do better next time. This set me trying to recall, not for the first time, what Christmas has meant to me over the years. First of all, growing up in the war with all the restrictions and rationing, it really was a time of celebration, beginning with somebody climbing in to the attic to retrieve a dusty box containing moth-eaten streamers and the odd bit of tarnished tinsel. With any luck we were able to supplement these with coloured strips of paper, painting twigs with whitening and sticking them into plasticine pots.

We always made the long journey from Weston-super-Mare to my Grandparents in Bristol where we squeezed into their tiny house buzzing with excitement. Joined by lots of cousins, we played party games and dressed up to present our own pantomime to the grown-ups. One year my Dad (home on leave from the RAF) fell ill with shingles and I cried a lot.

I have no memories of my teens but later as a nurse in Rochester, we sang carols in the Cathedral and round the Hospital, decorated the wards and entertained the patients with a pantomime. Then a spell in Africa where, because we lived in the Bush, there was no focus. It was very hot and life consisted of surviving each day so Christmas was low profile.

Back in England, work revolved round Borstals and Prisons with plenty of opportunity to introduce my Christian faith, and ideas of service, sharing and caring. With limited resources and obvious security restrictions, we still managed to implement outreach initiatives with some surprising outcomes.

When I was suddenly single again, divorced with a grown-up family, I was not allowed to spend Christmas alone, so experienced all sorts of festive seasons. People were very kind but I often felt like the stranger at the feast and lonely even in a crowd. Eventually, I declared independence and one Christmas Day in Birmingham, I shared my sandwich lunch in the park with the squirrels, cycled along the tow path and chatted to a dope smoking Rastafarian, then had a game of football in the street with a group of teenage Muslims. I have been to Ireland for religious devotion and in Australia declined an invitation to provide turkey and plum pudding in sweltering heat, but did enjoy dressing the tree and going to Church.

I feel great sadness at the commercialisation of Christmas. That people feel compelled to spend money they cannot afford on goods they do not need and often for those they would rather not see. It seems hypocritical to wrap up presents with resentment and send hundreds of cards for no good reason, when for the rest of the year, out of sight is out of mind. May I make a plea that we rethink this festive season. Put Jesus at the top of our present list, let Him into our lives and pray for guidance on how He would like us to celebrate His birth, not just this month, but throughout the year.

Happy Christmas, everyone, whatever you do, wherever you are.

Storms: Apocryphal and Personal

It was Autumn 1958 just a few weeks after Roger and I had met, and we were already engaged. I was walking on air. We loved ballroom dancing and it was on a rare Saturday when I was off duty at 5.30 p.m. but, on pain of death, obliged to be back at work at 7.30 a.m. next day. Social arrangements had to be made well ahead and could not easily be changed as the only point of contact was the public telephone call box in the Nurses' Home where I lived and the chance of getting a message at the last minute, pretty slim.

Roger was on leave from his job as a diamond prospector in West Africa, and staying at his parents' home in Sevenoaks, about 35 mins drive away. He was due to pick me up from the Nurses' Home at Rochester at 7 p.m. for the 30 min drive to Sidcup to join up with his siter, Jill, and husband to dance the night away.

October weather can be rough and this day was no exception. The leaves were coming off the trees, no match for the swirling wind and lashing rain, which made visibility poor and driving conditions hazardous. No matter, we set off in high spirits in our vintage car, large, imposing, no roof but plenty of height and bulk for protection. Roger, a man for all seasons, paratrooper, glider pilot, deep sea diver, rally driver, was in complete command.

We eventually arrived at our destination only to find the event cancelled due to damage to the building and flying debris giving rise to caution. It was decided to make haste to Jill and Mick's house nearby as the storm was gathering force. Safe inside, relieved, we put the kettle on and then realised flood water was pouring through the closed doors, rapidly getting deeper. As fast as possible we grabbed essentials and went upstairs, anxiously watching from the windows as anything not secured, was floating down the street and disappearing into darkness as street lights flickered and died.

Bearing in mind that society in the 1950s had a strict protocol and upstairs was the preserve of married couples and their offspring, so finding myself closeted in a bedroom with three comparative strangers, whatever the reason, was, to say the least, not admissible. Not known for toeing the line or being conventional, it made me giggle and I made a note to myself to share this secret with my adored father with whom I had a special bond and I knew would understand.

The flood water receded and although the storm still raged, Roger decided the priority was to get me back to the Nurses' Home, some 25 miles distant, before the deadline for my late pass at midnight expired. We tried various routes but all were blocked by floods, debris and fallen trees, so we decided, as they were away and we were passing by, to take refuge in Roger's parents' house. He assured me his sister, Lynda, would not mind me sleeping in her bed. My main concern was that I had no way of contacting Night Sister (only land lines existed and they were all down) so, even if I could get back for duty at 7.30 a.m. next day, I would still be put on matron's report that would unjustifiably add to other minor reprimands already on my record.

Mercifully, overnight the wind had abated and the rain ceased but there was still no guarantee that the roads would be passable. As we left the house at 6 a.m. the nosy parker neighbour opened her back door, peered at us with profound disapproval, pointed an accusatory finger and announced that she would make sure "young man, that your mother is duly informed that you have taken advantage of the situation and been entertaining a young lady overnight!". We smiled politely and drove away, happy and totally invulnerable whatever the consequences. The roads were clear enough and we made good time. Just for once, I was excused a bad report from the powers that be.

Honeymoon

Another storm I recall vividly, many years later, was in Downderry when I made an attempt to emulate my heroine, Grace Darling, and tried to retrieve a small boat that, having broken loose from its moorings, was being washed from the beach in off-shore gale force winds. I completely underestimated the strength needed and had not noticed the absence of any other help. Luckily a hefty seaman appeared as if by magic and he effortlessly hauled me and the boat to safety, so all ended happily.

However, I have absolutely no recall whatsoever of the violent extra tropical cyclone of October 1987 that ruthlessly ravaged the UK. That weekend, my personal world was ripped apart when Roger announced, without preamble or allowing time for debate, that he was leaving our marriage. No storm, however severe, could come close to matching that. I am glad I am a survivor.

Haircare

"There's a lot of it about." They say,
"no – not again"; day after day
It's not my fault, I do my bit
It's up to them; I'm sick of it!

Nitwit, lousy, dirty child,
All these names just make me wild.
Lice prefer the nice clean heads
To make their cosy little beds.

Next to the scalp, behind the ears
That's where you find the little dears,
So brush and comb and comb and brush
Take time, you can't afford to rush.

When you get the special stuff
Once overnight is quite enough.
When morning comes, just wash it out.
And seek advice if you're in doubt.

Each day before you come to school
Good grooming first; make it a rule
Help us help you, avoid the fuss
And make the headlice get rid of US.

To Live and Learn

Whilst never actually admitting to the feeling of total failure, I have often had to come to terms with the fact that there are an awful lot of people who are very much more clever at doing an awful lot more things than I shall ever have the time or inclination to tackle.

At school that 1st XI place I longed for never materialised, and on the academic front, my friends waltzed home with armfuls of cups and prizes. Later, I was very happy during eight years of nursing but never had any illusions that I was a 2nd Florence. Now I am a wife and mother of three children, I don't envy anyone.

Or do I? How can SHE make those delicious pasties when mine are all burnt pastry and raw meet? What about the lampshades another friend produces so easily? How does this one make her garden look so attractive all year round? And just think of the wallpapering and house painting my neighbour does. The heavenly smell of fresh baked bread makes me want to rush home and get up to my elbows in dough.

Somehow, I am always up to my eyes in sewing jobs instead. Not only knees out of trousers, or too short, but making a skirt out of that dress we found at the jumble sale last week; the left-over bits look well on the doll. One of the girls needs a ballet dress and really that coat is AWFUL! The lining is falling out of Father's favourite sports coat and my brother sends an SOS for a tweed cloak to keep him warm. (He's a shepherd in the French mountains and the nights are cold and long!)

All at once my friends want help with their sewing and in return I cadge tips for soft furnishings, baking, raising plants from seed and a host of other things. Not that all my efforts are successful by any means, and so often I come face to face with disaster that the family will say "Never mind, at least it tastes OK even if it looks awful!". Or, as I scramble round looking for things to put in a collage: "What in Heaven's name is that going to be?". I get the feeling that, even if they can write their names in the dust on the furniture, and there is often an awful scramble for the iron before we can depart on a promised outing, they always know I'll be at home when they come back, doing something … though what exactly is anybody's guess!

The Kendrick Family 1966

Faith, Hope and Patience

When they were small, my children were very enthusiastic members of the Sunday School, although, with the benefit of hindsight, I suspect it might have been more about being stars of the show with their friends on occasions in Big Church than anything to do with Biblical learning.

My husband's chosen profession meant we moved houses and locations frequently so we had the interesting experience of living all over England. One sad vicar positively discouraged all children and young people as, in his eyes they demanded too much attention and were a distraction from the serious business of worship. We tried hard but failed to change his mind and, sadly, turned away disappointed, disillusioned but determined not to be defeated. We soon found somewhere else.

Later, we lived in Cornwall where all spare time blurred into busy activity, mostly focussed on the beach whatever the weather and where calendars and clocks had no place. Luckily, the booming chapel bell scythed through all howling winds, crashing waves and sounds of silence, and as soon as we heard it, the whole village raced up the street just as we were. There was always a scramble for the best seats to hear the powerful words of the minister, majestic in flowing black robes and long white hair with curly bits at the end, looking like John Wesley. He inspired all ages. We sang lustily, listened avidly, prayed earnestly and then went home excited and motivated for the week ahead.

A move to Brixton in South London was a rude awakening and my two older children soon found alternative interests which did not include attending Sunday services. My youngest, then nine years old, faithfully and happily joined me and a maximum of five other congregants - average age seventy – in the massive Victorian, red brick church where each week we huddled together in dim lighting with warm clothes which in winter we augmented with blankets and hot water bottles. Inevitably, the building had to close and became a warehouse. We moved next door to the school room which proved popular and numbers increased considerably.

As adults, none of my children resumed regular worship or Church membership and I have had to learn to accept that my only grandchild has never been christened, something I deeply regret. I used to include gentle reminders in letters to them wherever they were in the world, but was politely asked to refrain and, of course respected that. They are, after all, good kind thoughtful, considerate, caring people and Christianity is not limited to church walls. We are commissioned to be patient as "God works in mysterious ways His wonders to perform" and in the past, I have petulantly dumped things at the foot of the cross and left them there in desperation only to find, later, that matters have been quietly resolved without the input which I considered to be essential.

Journey with Faith

I have never courted change or been interested in dangerous activities that included high risk or great speed, much preferring bats and balls and books. So, when my adored father presented me with a bicycle for my eighth birthday, I sensed something had to give. It was war time and everything was in short supply. I knew it must have taken him many months to save up enough money from his meagre wage and I wanted to please him. I pretended to be over the moon, though my heart was breaking at the thought of the unrequited sacrifice and the feat I had to overcome to avoid his disappointment.

My brother, four years older, had a hold on life, instinctively understood and immediately insisted on taking me to the dirt track behind our house where we would be safe from the prying eyes of nosy neighbours and protective parents. He was a role model and a good teacher and I had faith that, if I listened and obeyed his instructions, all would be well. Once he had explained the principles of balance v propulsion (which I pretended to understand), I got on, settled myself fearfully, made sure my feet could easily touch *terra firma* whilst my bottom hovered hesitantly over the solid saddle and felt a sense of foreboding tinged with excitement. My brother was gentle and firm, assuring me that he would not let me go until I was safe. All I needed to do was look forward, aim for the hedge in the far distance and pedal hard, not thinking about anything else except the finish.

Once mobile, at what seemed a mighty pace, I made the mistake of looking back, found he had already let me go and promptly fell off with a mighty bang, skidding along the rough ground with my dignity in tatters. No other damage done, and he was adamant that we do it again, and again, and again until I was sailing solo at least in a straight line, staying upright and stopping short of any solid barriers.

Though other interests later jostled for supremacy, that introduction to cycling stood me in good stead, especially in my teenage years, when I could gratefully disappear all daylong on my own with just light refreshments and solitude for company.

As time went by, I never forgot that day and it became a firm foundation stone, a solid reference point, a simple starting place for difficult situations. A salutary lesson that anything is possible when we share and care enough to respond to circumstances, listen to advice and make informed choices, mindful that every action has a reaction. Our journey through life has a beginning over which we have no control. If we are fortunate, we may influence things towards the end. What is important is the way we cover the ground in the middle. Faith is a good companion.

Reluctant Pupil

I was never interested in being closeted in a classroom and have no idea how I came to win a scholarship to Weston-super-Mare Girls' Grammar School. On the day of the entry exams, I managed to knock myself unconscious whilst running amok in the playground during break time. It was 1947, just before the NHS made us all dependent on hospitals and long before Health and Safety made everybody nervous about litigation, so I was revived by cold water sponging and briefly rested before being propped up at a desk to carry on with the rest of the tests.

The following year, having been awarded a major scholarship, I made my way, alone, across town by bus, to join dozens of other girls from a wide area, also on the cusp of secondary education. Dressed identically in smart uniforms complete with velour hats, we all had obligatory sports bags and equipment, and in my brown satchel was a present from my master carpenter grandfather: a gold-coloured tin containing a ruler, pencil, set square, protractor and (although only one) something called a pair of compasses. Although I never took maths seriously, I did love drawing diagrams and writing mystic theorems. When other lessons were boring, my attention wandered to the outside world and time stood still.

Whilst I was forever planning my escape from formal lessons, I had no idea that all my friends were actually studying really hard, getting good marks. Our teachers didn't seem to notice my lack of diligence or absence of homework, which was a relief, and it never occurred to me that being very near the bottom of the class was significant in the scheme of things. One exception was Miss Brice, well past her sell-by day in terms of appearance or eligibility in the marriage market, she was permanently dressed in drab tweeds, brown lisle stockings and brogues.

Even allowing for clothes rationing which was still in force, a small variation part of her outfit would have found favour. Having only once very publicly and deliberately singled me out as being "hopeless" – and whether or not it was a deliberate ploy I do not know – but it was a bait I swallowed, determined to prove her wrong.

Her penetrating voice and fixed stare from behind pebble glasses commanded immediate attention and earned my reluctant respect. She taught us English and my friends and I spent many hours under her direction that resulted in elaborate productions of Shakespeare plays on very meagre budgets. She had a way of making grammar interesting and language alluring, dissecting such words as onomatopoeia, encouraging description alliteration, putting past participles in their place, making verbs, nouns and adjectives exciting extras. Not much use outside school, but I was quite happy absorbed in the energy of our spoken language whilst my friends concentrated with dogged determination on sciences, languages, history and the world.

At 16, as they all clutched their collections of certificates and medals and stayed on for further pursuit of knowledge and academic acclaim, I was happy to end my school days there and then, with qualification in English Literature and Domestic Science and the secret satisfaction that, unlike them, I had enjoyed and excelled in playing hockey, netball and tennis. I was also now free to devote more time to amateur theatricals and sport whilst earning a small wage and enjoying life in the fast lane to the future. I have no regrets.

Treasure Trove

Two whistles, a pencil, a ball and a stone
A pen top a rubber a thing for the phone
Blutack, a magnet, a coin and a die
All might be useful some day, by and by

Screws and a cup hook, a chain and some chalk,
Tweezers, a watch spring, an old flower stalk.
Odd earrings and till bills, notes out of date
Seeds in a packet - I've left them too late!

This tray is a treasure I'd save in a flood
(There's a tie for a tourniquet to stop any blood!)
I know, it's quite certain, without any doubt.
There's nothing of value, but I can't throw it out!

The Last Furlong

The road is one of ups and downs in a constantly changing landscape from absolute despair and loneliness to hope and reassurance. From galloping down a race track of abandoned self in perpetual turmoil to a gentle stroll through spring meadows filled with perfumed relaxation.

Dashing over hedges and ditches in a blind panic to an uncertain future is a solitary journey and scary, but cuddly toys are comforting, constant and understanding companions, able to quietly absorb disturbing thoughts and destructive fears.

Molehills can be managed. Mountains are best left as a distant vista, inspiring and panoramic, but where climbers, concentrating solely on the next step, are constantly challenged to the point of physical and mental exhaustion.

At worst, death for those left behind is the total elimination of the body shell and an empty chair.

At best for our loved ones, it is eternal life, free from earthly constraints and pain, with time to rest til we meet again on an island of peace in a sea of tranquillity. Heaven!

Travel to the ends of the Earth

Highdays and Holidays

I would have loved to have gone to Lamborene to be a nurse in the leper colony. The flying Doctor service in Australia caught my imagination or even being a farmer's wife in the English countryside, in a cottage with roses round the door, chickens in the yard and a dairy where I could make butter to put on the homemade bread ...

In no time at all, it seems, I have had my three score years and ten, a full life of different experiences and adventure and have just got back to Base Camp (home) from perhaps the most exciting and challenging one.

Growing up in the war, books were scarce, and TV nonexistent so we listened a lot to the Radio and story tellers and used our fertile imagination to picture the exploits of brave people who dared to go where mere mortals would not venture. News blackouts meant we only had snatches of information about the battles for Britain, although that was enough for a 6-year-old to get really excited. But there were wonderful tales about Scott and the Endeavour and his ultimate demise which seemed even more alluring. Another seed was sewn.

Over the last two years, my younger daughter, living in Australia, and I have looked at Antarctica with great interest, but decided even with modern transport it was too much travelling time for me. So, we opted to go North to the High Arctic. Flying to Longyearben via Oslo and Tromso, we boarded the good ship "Polar Pioneer" with 50 passengers, and over 12 days covered thousands of sea miles and reached 80 degrees N and 18 degrees 11' East.

Arctic holiday Jennifer

Twenty-four-hour sunshine made sleeping patterns erratic and there was often a call just as you got settled on your bunk for a snooze. We saw polar bears of all sizes, walruses, huge and so cumbersome but harmless unless they accidentally squashed you. Whales of every kind though sadly no tails in the air, puffins, kittiwakes, fulmars and terns, reindeer, seals and exquisite flora it was impossible not to tread on when we went walking on the tundra.

We cruised on Zodiacs into remote places where the sound of calving glaciers was like fat in a hot frying pan. My daughter and her friends kayaked and did a polar plunge (jumping from the ship into the icy water) and have certificates to prove it. I am told we are officially expeditioners, having hiked in extreme areas where armed guards (hunky Vikings including one female) were obligatory in case of a surprise meeting with a big beastie.

Incidentally, en route, we also went to my elder daughter's wedding in Scotland which was another joyful day with a few special people to celebrate and indelible memories to add to our bank. Now, I am in recovery and so thankful for the opportunity to see so much of God's wonderful world, but mindful of how fragile it is.

Polar Bears may be extinct in 45 years due to the accumulation of flame retardants in the food chain. That's scary.

Australia 2000

Despite all my research and (pretend) self-assurance before leaving, I had no idea what an enormous and steep learning curve I was embarking on as I was taken to Heathrow in a howling gale and lashing rain at the end of October. *Tomorrow is another Time Zone* – so the following day disappeared completely and the plane touched down in beautiful sunshine at 6am

Perth time where the city was already busy, the hotel ready and welcoming and with a full-size swimming pool – *no drama* as the Aussies say.

Despite lack of sleep, I hopped on the FREE bus to explore the city and found my way round easily so that by the next day when I met my eight travelling companions and our leader for our three weeks by mini bus, it was all OK. It soon became apparent how vast this continent is as despite driving 3,000 miles we made very little impact on the map, spending hours on long, straight roads seeing nothing but emus and kangaroos before suddenly meeting a 'phone box, gas station and coffee stop. Extraordinary!

Since I began planning this in 1999, I have always known that the Lord's hand was on the helm and everywhere we went felt like a pilgrimage – but a two-way process as we were able to give as well as receive to the obvious benefit of all. Our accommodation was varied from a motel, to a converted hospital, an old loco shed in the forest, to a very upmarket ocean-side hotel where we had smoked salmon and caviar for breakfast.

We learned to take nothing for granted. That stick could be a snake, spiders bite and even a friendly kanga can pack a mighty punch – and whilst out in a small boat, I was lucky enough to see an 80ft blue whale that even had the skipper excited. I swam a little anxiously due to the undertow in a bay busy with trippers, not knowing that a shark was lurking in the shallows and would take a man's life soon after. It makes one realise how very precious life is.

One night we were taken by an Aboriginal for a bush barby in the moonlight. He had been badly treated at school by missionaries and ended up on drugs and in crime. He married very young and 'divorced'. Much later he prayed that God would send him an Abo woman who would help him 'do good'. His prayers were answered but not in the way he asked. She is an educated white lady who is Roman Catholic. God certainly works in mysterious ways!

On Remembrance Sunday I found myself alone (we had a free day) so with poppies in my raffia hat, I sat at a busy road junction and had two minutes solitary silence whilst the rest of the world rushed by. I might do that in England another year, except that it could be cold and wet.

Morning service in Albany was great as they had well known hymns and we were able to augment the wheezy musical machine with joyful praise which pleased everyone. It was a surprise to hear them praying for us in the UK and brought us nearer to home. Not so easy in Sydney where, as directed by the Notice Board, I turned up for a 7pm service to find the door locked. The house next door was filling up but people were too busy happy clapping to see a stranger at the door with no handle on the outside. I shed the dust from my feet and walked on.

FINE FOOD IN SYDNEY HARBOURSIDE.

Fish from the market, herbs dressed in oil,
Potatoes in the saucepan coming up to boil.
Fish in the grill pan, herbs tossed around,
Potatoes mashed with butter, salt and pepper ground.
Fish all crispy, brown and gold, herbs sparkly and green,
Potatoes soft and fluffy white, placed with pride on a tureen.
A simple meal, a pretty plate, food prepared with care,
Fresh fish and herbs and seasoned spuds, a feast beyond compare.

Family Fun Days

Supposing people are wondering if I have disappeared down a mud slide or been lost without trace, I am pleased to say that I have had three months staying with my scattered family in Australia. November, December and January are their summer/autumn days so very hot and humid in Queensland and New South Wales and we spent Christmas up in the mountains, sitting under the canopy of rain forest in my son's garden, the trees suitably decorating with tinselly trimmings. A plentiful supply of fresh fish, fruit and salads was complemented by plum pudding but the fruit cake I made was a disaster.

The local church was welcoming and 'busy' with a vicar very much out of Janet Bromley's mould, so we had a lot of fun and spiritual worship, including one Blue Christmas weekday service for those who were lonely, sad or otherwise in need. It was a new innovation and few people turned up, but it was a great idea and to be encouraged.

Commuting 1,000 miles by train and plane between Brisbane and Sydney is easy, so I have done it a few times and had the best of both worlds. My daughter and I were happy hooligans at the Big Bash Cricket at the Sydney Cricket Ground twice which was exciting and we also went for champagne breakfast at the Opera House one day. I had to pinch myself to believe it as we sat on the terrace up close and personal to the Harbour Bridge in genteel company, by invitation only!

As I write, this is my last day and I am enjoying wall to wall blue sky and a gentle breeze off the ocean sitting on the balcony at my daughter's apartment. A helicopter hovers overhead issuing a shark alert, reminding me that even in paradise there are hazards, something I found out recently when a monster munchy thing (probably a spider but it didn't introduce itself for identification so we'll never know) bit me and made me proper poorly.

England has much to offer too, as Bill Bryson illustrates so graphically in his book *Notes from a Small Island*. I am so blessed to have travelled and be back home!

More News from Down Under

Sizzling Sydney! City streets have plenty of trees but I have not been tempted further than the little beach on the river just down the road from our temporary home. It was allegedly one of the earliest settlements where an enterprising convict grew hops and set up an enormous brewery. This then became a Mecca and watering hole for more of the same. Now just a derelict site, it is still possible to sit under the mango trees, watch the water flow by and reflect on history.

Yesterday, Frankie drove us 90 minutes out into the real country typified in books and illustrations of this great place. And there, in the middle of nothing, appeared a huge cereal mill, silver in the sun, looking like a benign gorilla waiting for food. Another few miles and a small town which boasts a modest Thomas the Tank Engine Museum and other essential supplies plus a dear little, desperately neglected house that had had a period as a hippy commune and is now being renovated by Frankie and friends. I loved it, but am concerned about the amount of work yet to be done in their spare time and on an ever-shrinking budget.

In the overgrown garden, evidence of an abundance of fabulous flowers just longing to be set free and a sight of my first honey eater – a tiny little bird enjoying the nectar – and the relatively wild surroundings. Then, as I sat on the front deck, behind the picket fence, I saw something moving in the road miraculously being missed by fast moving vehicles. A grass cutting machine had earlier pulled out of the grounds opposite and when I managed to rescue the creature, it turned out to be a turtle/tortoise that looked as if it had been flattened in the field, possibly stuck to the tyre and bumped off. Not a happy chappy, but thankfully, all the soft bits were intact so I put him back in the bush by a trickle of water and he soon disappeared to safety. All creatures great and small ...

Frankie's House

Easter Greetings from Australia

As I write this in early March, the temperature is in the mid-30s and the humidity so high that even Sydneysiders are feeling the heat. I have spent time this week with a Catholic family. Grandparents, parents and five children who live side by side in a small community surrounded by bush land, an hour's drive north of the city.

Theirs is an incredibly busy life from the basics of school runs and umpteen other activities that young ones are involved in, to many roles in the local parish and the maintenance of the acres round the house. Every household has a swimming pool, of course, maybe a tennis court and nearly always chickens and dogs. Each day the fences have to be checked for damage by kangaroos and all precautions taken to reduce fire risk. Everything is tinder dry. If you stand still long enough, you see lizards (great at keeping the mosquito population down) and lots of parrots and other exotic birds. There was a refreshing air of caring and sharing as we did the chores – many hands really do make light work – and talked about God's wonderful world.

I have also been to Canberra, the capital of Australia, and a lovely city of wide-open green spaces and long straight avenues. I was lucky to meet a delightful Israeli Jew who patiently and gently answered lots of questions, so I have been able to learn a little at first hand about their situation. To be truthful, I shall be glad to get home and give my brain a rest. There is so much going on, but I give thanks to God each day that I am able to travel so far and see so much.

Guidance and Light

Visiting my daughter in Sydney for the first time, I was pleased to see a Church immediately opposite her apartment. True, the path was rough and bushes crowded round the door making it look neglected, but I had no trouble in finding information about Sunday Services from the noticeboard near the road.

When the time came, bright lights beamed from all the windows, showing crowds of people gathering, talking and laughing. I carefully picked my way to the door, only to find there was no handle or knocker on the outside, so I rapped firmly on the window. People looked, saw me and turned away. Nobody came, so eventually and sadly, I gave up, shook the dust from my heels and left.

During the following week, I came across another very different Church building with a proud banner announcing "UNDER NEW MANAGEMENT" accompanied by a variety of dates and times for all sorts of meetings, activities and services. However, when I turned up at the time appointed for Morning Prayer, there was nobody there, so I checked the board and returned later for Evensong. Still the place was locked, barred and bolted. Nobody came!

A few days later, I was walking round the maze of back streets and got hopelessly lost. Daylight was fading fast. I had no money or mobile phone on me and suddenly felt alone and vulnerable. Something made me aim for a plain white wall shining like a beacon at the far end of the empty street. As I got nearer, I could hear voices and as the front door was ajar, decided to go in and ask for help.

Everyone was so friendly and assured me that, in fact I was only round the corner from where my daughter lived. I stayed for coffee and refreshments and left with a warm invitation to join them for Sunday worship which I did for the rest of my three month stay. The fellowship was stimulating, fun and spiritual and I shall always be grateful to them and the way the Lord guided me there.

Picnic by Sydney Bridge

Mum's Marathon

"By the way, Mum", said my daughter as she met me at the end of my 24-hour flight from London to Sydney, "when you go to Brisbane, remind me there is a carpet to go with you."

A week later I was back at Kingsford Smith airport carrying minimal personal belongings to make it easier to cope with the large heavy roll of Persian rug. The unseasonal rain hammered down as we drove to the parking lot, ducking under low hovering helicopters and running the gauntlet of dozens of uniformed police. It was only as we passed close to a smartly attired plane with elegant passengers hiding under huge black umbrellas as they made their way down the red carpet that we remembered that Prince Charles was in town! To complicate things further, we later discovered that the airport computer checking-in system had broken down and nobody else was going anywhere.

We spent the rest of the day trying to think of ways of losing the excess baggage, and there were plenty of jibes about magic carpets and flying – all of which lightened the gloom but did nothing practical to help the dire situation. After much to-ing and fro-ing, littered with confusing information, it was a great relief to finally get clearance and see the wretched thing move along and disappear down a chute. I really didn't care if it never resurfaced.

The plane looked small and friendly as I crossed the tarmac and climbed the steps, so much more exciting than boarding through a shabby tunnel, and I settled happily in my window seat for the short hop up the coast. Daylight saving between NSW and Queensland meant we arrived before we had taken off!

The tropical storm still raged as we landed 90 minutes later, but the rain was warm and the drenching a welcome relief from the humid heat. Once inside the airport, I could see the carpet sitting smug and dry, as it was first off the plane onto the carousel, and I felt a secret self-satisfaction as if I had been an unlikely medal winner in a marathon. It is now laid in my son's old colonial home, the most recent addition to an eclectic collection of possessions representing various stages of his life from childhood, alongside numerous more domestic antiques and pretty sentimental treasures of her own that his wife has lovingly displayed. A joy to behold and worth all the effort, but I am in no hurry to be a courier again, unless the goods weigh nothing and will fit neatly in my handbag.

God Always Answers

It had taken many years and a lot of not very gentle persuasion, for me to agree to allow an iPad to enter my life. I did have a fax machine under sufferance a long while ago, which was quickly outdated and old fashioned according to the daughter who will be obeyed and was replaced by a computer which I tolerated for a quiet life.

It should be made clear that as a long-time solo survivor enjoying a full life of independence, I saw no need for gadgets and gizmos getting in the way or taking up valuable space in my head and home. Even a mobile phone was for emergency use only, often left lurking in coat pockets or other places not regularly visited but generally located by a process of patient elimination. Eventually in a brave stand of open defiance, I got rid of my TV and computer and managed happily, reading and writing (printed books and pen and paper still worked very well for me) for more than five years, not feeling in the least bit deprived.

Then, when I was planning yet another trip to visit my daughter living in Sydney, she suggested I might look at the latest model of PCs on the market which were all singing and dancing wonders and would be cheaper at the airport. Being a dutiful parent, I did as I was bidden and was persuaded by a most charming salesman, to buy one. I spent the rest of the journey regretting it, but when I arrived and my daughter offered to relieve me of the burden, I sensed subterfuge and decided to keep if for myself with no intention of ever letting it see the light of day.

Back in UK once more, I began to dabble with this new toy and found it did extraordinary things, didn't cause pain or get cross, take up precious space or make unnecessary demands on me and so we became firm friends. Time went on and eventually, but reluctantly I ventured into the realms of seeing my daughter on screen for talks which have now become a weekly ritual that I really look forward to, especially as I can no longer travel so don't see her as often in person.

Recently she looked weary and admitted to feeling tired, but in Australia they work hard from early morning to mid-afternoon and spend the rest of the day and all weekends at the beach, actively taking part in, or being involved with, anything sporty. I was concerned that she was doing too much. And so it was that I earnestly prayed that she would slow down just a bit, mindful of her 52-year-old body occasionally needing rest and recovery time.

A fortnight later she broke her toe really badly (at home, with bare feet, bumped into furniture in the dark) and although not totally immobile, was in a lot of pain, in a surgical boot and unable to swim or do much exercise for five weeks. Mercifully she was able to travel to UK for Christmas as planned and we have just had the most wonderful week pottering around gently catching up with family and friends who managed to include Dursley in their itineraries up and down the country whilst we held open house.

God always answers our prayers, but quite often in unexpected ways. I am so thankful for his mercy and have a feeling He will be smiling to himself, satisfied at his resolution to this particular prayer.

Just Smile

Coming only a few days after I had spent two months catching up with my offspring in Australia, enjoying long days of sunshine and activity, I knew that Christmas back in UK would be very different. Consequently, I had deliberately arranged with my cousin to go and stay in a Premier Inn on a busy motorway junction in Staffordshire for the festivities. No unnecessary frills, but bright, clean comfortable accommodation.

A few miles away a canalside pub was warm and welcoming, providing all our food and simple entertainment needs. Likewise, Lichfield Cathedral met our spiritual needs and a visit to the National Memorial Arboretum realised a long-held ambition with plenty of time and space to quietly reflect, rejoice and be truly thankful on so many levels. Mission accomplished!

It was a surprise when, shortly afterwards, back home and alone once more, that I suddenly felt compelled to shut off from the world. It was as if the safety curtain had come down at the end of a gala performance, leaving me abandoned on an empty stage. Like Alice in Nowhere Land, I was fearlessly free-falling in a dark swirling space with no reference to reality and roughly rejected a friend's kind offer of help, grateful that they understood and did not persist.

I lived on porridge and fruit for a week which satisfied my appetite, (after all Africans eat little else) and spent much time sleeping naturally, quite content in the possibility that I might not wake up. That would be neat and tidy.

Eventually, I dragged myself to the Epiphany Evensong Carol Service at St Mark's which felt like a trickle of warm water that slowly started to thaw the ice floes surrounding me. Walking home that evening deep in thought, I was briefly greeted by the bright, smiling face of a stranger going the other way, a switch flicked and the thaw was hastened by a faint glimmer of hope that slowly began to sparkle and gradually glowed like firelight. I am so grateful to that person whose smile was genuine and whose greeting made no demands but left a trail of loving kindness in its wake and a spring in my step.

Angels appear out of the blue, often in unexpected guises and may be totally unaware of the effect they have. Anyone can be part of that throng. Just smile, though your heart is breaking, it could be the kiss of life …

Powers of Destruction

Whatever happened to Ethel with her shawl and snowy-
white hair,
Who sat by the fire and knitted as she rocked in her old
Windsor chair?
Friends Betty and Vera lived one side and Harry and Alice
next door,
Daisy and Fred, Nelly and Bob were opposite at two three
and four.
Along came some strangers with clipboards and
powerfully swept them aside,
"Don't worry, m'darlin's" they bellowed, "We're taking
you all for a ride!".
They'd hired a coach for these people and drove them ten
miles across town.
The old folk were weary and worried: "What's this?" they
all said with a frown.
"New flats" said the strangers so proudly, determined to
make their scheme pay,
Not minding what personal sorrow was caused at the end
of the day.
A matter of only weeks later, removers returned to their
street,
"Right-o, m'luvvers, you ready to go? You know them
new homes'll suit you a treat."
In no time, bulldozers flattened the neighbourhood where
the old folk had been.
No-one considered just what was destroyed as they crazily
exercised power at the scene,
Nor cared that in one easy movement irreparable damage
was done
As a close-knit community was shattered and decades of
shared living was gone.

Health and Safety

Silly Girl

A busy week was rudely, suddenly and unexpectedly interrupted when I became another statistic on that endless register of accidents that happen at home. A wine glass that I was, unwisely now I accept, using as a pastry cutter shattered with an impressive explosion and left me with a huge hole in my hand. A moment of disbelief and confusion was quickly followed by the realisation that I needed immediate help. I was alone and a desperate look out of windows front and back only showed blank darkness as everyone had obviously gone to the moon! Just then, in answer to an arrow prayer, a light appeared in a house over the road and, as I ran down the garden path, my neighbour came to her door to put the rubbish out.

Back in my kitchen there were cakes in the oven, quince jelly on the stove, biscuit mixture in the process of being shaped and the general detritus of one of my rare marathon cooking sessions in preparation for forthcoming fundraising events. Nevertheless, together we hatched a plan, switched off the electrical appliances, picked up house keys and, in next to no time, I was loaded into her car.

Rush hour on a dark, wet and windy winter night is not the first choice for an unscheduled outing and it took an hour to get to casualty.

"Be thankful you didn't have to trek three days through the jungle!" said my friend, Kathy, dryly, which made me laugh and feel less vulnerable.

Once in hospital, It was established that I had, mercifully, missed tendons and arteries and the wound was plugged with something out of a tube and held together with strips of sticky stuff reminiscent of Blue Peter programmes. Next day, an ex-ray revealed glass still in the wound so I had an appointment to see the Hand Man who apparently operates in the fracture clinic – which is all a bit confusing.

No prizes for guessing what I am expecting in triplicate in my Christmas stocking. The moral of this story is to only use the proper utensils suited to the task and maybe UHU glue and Sellotape could be useful ingredients to include in a First Aid kit in the kitchen!

For the record, all the cooking miraculously survived and sold ... like hot cakes! Phew!

The Roller Coaster Ride

I met lots of new and really interesting people on the way. It was a journey I had not expected or prepared for so, as events unfolded, my head felt like the clothes in a tumble dryer, hot and mixed up and all over the place.

Having been in increasing pain for five days without relief from simple home remedies, it seemed sensible to go to the GP for comforting advice and maybe a prescription. To my surprise, she firmly and gently said I needed more urgent attention. The paramedics took over. No need for flashing blue lights and a siren, so as I lay in the ambulance relieved to be in safe hands, I had a grandstand view of passing traffic and it was a surprise that everything in the outside world was carrying on as normal when my life had suddenly turned turtle. I had visions of a tangled mass of wet knitting wool with no way of getting it sorted until the end is found as a way back to the beginning.

Fast track through Casualty was another new experience. Though I pretended to myself the speed was due to a lull in patient numbers at that moment in time, the imaginary surgeon's knife still dangled in front of my clouded vision like the sword of Damocles. By this time, I had forgotten to worry about things back in my empty, suddenly abandoned house. Had I made the bed? Laundry in the wash basket, dishes in the sink, fridge with leftover food … the list goes on but once I was tucked up on the ward in a crisp clean bed, pain free and woozy, nothing else mattered.

Plugged into various contraptions, I slept peacefully and an overnight test revealed the likely source of a virulent infection that a course of appropriate antibiotics would probably sort out without an operation. The consultant surgeon arrived for the ward round, accompanied by a long retinue of underlings neatly lined up in order of height and seniority. He had obviously modelled his manner on James Robertson Justice in *Doctor in the House*, the difference being his thin figure, clean-shaven face, sharp nose and empty eye sockets. Impatient and arrogant to the point of contempt he left me reeling, declaiming for all the ward to hear, that I was not in need of a bed and SHOULD GO!

He promptly departed trailing his team in his pompous wake, reminding me of a Commandant in a concentration camp. After a while, I was brave enough to negotiate with the Senior Nurse and stayed put, so imagine the Consultant's apoplexy next day to find me still there. This time I was ready, rested and recovering. He was shocked when I dared to speak and refused to be bullied. The good news is I survived, albeit mentally battered by one man's inhumanity to man, and I am deeply grateful for our National Health Service. I have now seen first hand examples of excellent practice coupled with fundamental far-reaching failings which could easily be remedied, some more complicated issues and a very few serious shortcomings which need urgent attention.

I hope to use this experience in a positive and practical way and find out, for example, why, at 75 years old and an independent solo survivor, I did not qualify for a day or two to recuperate at the community hospital but returned instead to an empty house, relying on busy neighbours for support. The best of all was the card I received from St James and St Mark's signed by so many well-wishers and which reminds me every day how blessed I am. Thank you so much, each and every one!

Helpful Hints about Being in Hospital

Be careful what you pray for. Love and attention was lacking in my life and I was not tempted by on-line lonely-hearts, come to mama, or speed dating all of which seemed to demand an element of commitment which was too demanding for a 79 soon to be 80 year old solo survivor.

The cavalry came to my house in the shape of a sparkly green and yellow chariot with blue lights and a paramedic whose persuasive powers took me swiftly but gently to A& E, feeling like Boudicca in need of a battery charge. The opposing force was galloping pneumonia and far too strong for me to overcome alone; not what I wanted or asked for.

Nevertheless, and despite constant reports and concrete evidence about our struggling NHS, I was soon tucked up in a hospital bed, on what felt like a metal magic carpet with buttons and umpteen knobs, and surrounded by all the elements of modern medical warfare. I was hooked up to a friendly machine that breathed for me and draped in the armour of drip wires and plastic tubing with a fetching face mask dispensing life-saving oxygen and the blessed relief of sleep.

A week later it seemed like a good idea to ask a uniformed volunteer to take me in a wheelchair to visit my friends in another ward. However, seeing the average age and state of health of the 'pram' pushers, I decided not to risk it.

As an emergency admission without any belongings, clad in a vivid pink hospital gown, any thoughts of an early escape soon vanish.

Moving house in an orderly fashion is one thing, but moving hospital wards in the middle of the night is an experience not to be recommended for the faint-hearted.

When it takes porters at a fast pace 15 minutes or more to get you to your new destination, you know you have gone some distance but are still in the confines of the hospital.

Hospital beds are like metal, magic carpets except that when you have one to use, you lack the mental capacity to find out how things work and the physical strength to put it into action.

If you are a mobile patient in hospital and get out of bed to go to the toilet in the middle of the night, remember to make a note of where you came from. All corridors look the same in institutions and the bigger the signs the less you see them.

Being an independently mobile patient on a hospital ward where the bathroom is set up for the elderly, mentally infirm proved interesting. The door was reluctant to shut first of all and the seat was set immediately under the shower head which allowed little flexibility but did fold up out of the way. There was an ordinary mixer mechanism for water, heat and power, all of which I was able to raise to suit me. Trouble was, this meant the water was not neatly contained as it would have been with a smaller body sitting on the seat, being tended to by an alert attendant behind the half screen. I was only aware of the great water escape when gingerly stepping out through the half doors of the little cubicle onto what I thought was dry land but was actually awash and making waves.

There was no cord connected to the alarm and I was not in a hurry to go in search of help down the corridor with only the briefest of outfits to cover me, and no confidence that I could walk unaided, so was unsure what to do. In the end, I mopped up a bit, put my head out of the door and hoped to catch sight of some help. In future, I will hunt for a better solution.

Sometimes We Need Help

It all began at the beginning of December. I had a dry tickly throat. Like everyone else in the land, I had a full diary of essential commitments and failing to fulfil each one was not an option whilst I was still able to walk and talk.

A week later I felt quite ill but still refused to give in, confident that I could cope alone ... who said that pride comes before a fall? My daughter phoned from Scotland and could hear my croaking voice and wheezy breathing and was adamant that I ask for help. I knew she was right but that first step was so hard.

I need not have worried as once the neighbours knew, they were only too pleased to do shopping, bring little treats and wave cheerily through the window to make sure I was OK. Then I had to make the phone calls to tell people that I was not available for things I had promised to do. Everyone was so supportive and understanding. To my surprise the sky did not fall in and I was able to retire to bed with pills from the Doctor and stayed there for four days.

It was a very different Christmas as I had time to think and pray, surrounded by cards and letters but without the distraction of over-eating, over-spending and rushing about that can so often detract from the real meaning of this festive season. Now my energy levels are restored and I am able to think things over, I feel thankful and richer for the experience.

Yet again I am in awe at the wonderful ways our Lord has of working things out and am only sorry that I personally make his life so hard. It reminds me constantly of my relationship with my earthly father and **his** unconditional love ... I feel doubly blessed.

My Father

Thank you, my Patient

Is it not in a way rather sad
That we should have met as we did?
It could, I admit, have been very much worse –
You were the patient and I was your nurse.

I fell at once for your charming ways
(my feelings deepened in the following days)
Then came the time for you to go
I bid you goodbye (How? I don't know.)

That day was so long, I tried to work hard.
But I thought of you as I came on the ward.
You've no idea what it meant to me
To help to nurse a person like you.

People take for granted the work we do –
"Do this", "Do that" is all they can say,
In such an offhand, bossy way.
It makes a difference, a cheerful face,
Makes work worthwhile, time flies at a pace;
Days come and go, weeks in, weeks out.
We don't notice time as we hurry about.

Please God, may there be more like you
I do not ask for any reward,
Except a word or occasional smile –
That makes our work seem more worthwhile.

Thank you for being so kind to us
You went away without any fuss.
May your friends treat you as you treated me

During those few days you happened to be
In a hospital bed on St William's Way.

I trust you'll never again have to stay
Within four walls of a white-washed ward,
But if you should, you may rest assured,
Just keep smiling and try to have a kind word.
You'll find love and respect and your health restored.

Second Chance

In 1993 and without any warning, I was diagnosed
with cancer. It was a shock and I tried to explain to
the Doctor that I did not feel ill, had no visible alien
lumps or bumps and had no time to be off sick.
True, I was very weary due to a heavy workload and
attempts to get out of debt following an acrimonious
divorce a long time before, but I had no free time and
far too much to do to be idle in bed.   I won my case
and carried on seven days a week convinced that I
was absolutely infallible and certainly indispensable.
How arrogant was that!

It could have so easily ended in disaster, but one day
my Doctor peered over his pince-nez and gently, but
firmly informed me that I was being very unwise. It
stopped me in my tracks and I was allowed just
enough time to find a guardian for my precious
pussycat before I was admitted to Hospital for a
major rebuild.   After surgery, I lay helplessly

attached to all manner of mechanical things, feeling trapped and confused, but strangely calm amidst the mayhem. Then I herd the Lord's voice: "You could have died. Now LIVE!".

Recovery was long, slow and frustrating. For many months I was totally dependent on others as I had no reserves of mental or physical energy and needed regular chemotherapy. Very gradually, the fog began to clear and I started to see the world in much more detail. Everything was beautiful, everyone helped me find my feet and my life began again. Since then, I have made great efforts to balance things sensibly. Sometimes I sits and thinks … sometimes, I just sit!

I hope I may be forgiven for seeing this whole experience as a my personal crucifixion, death and resurrection. Each day, I thank the Lord for His presence, ask for His guidance and wonder if I am worthy of His love. Perhaps He thinks "could do better" and I promise I will try. Easter is a good time to take stock, with lots of opportunities to reflect in silence, before the joyous celebrations. May God bless the world with new sight, concern for each other and Peace.

Home Communion

Three months of being confined to barracks, suddenly reduced to helplessness so soon after returning from a long and very active stay in Australia, has offered up a whole raft of new experiences. Most of them, like help with being showered and fed, were not an optional extra but absolutely essential and, although the caring and considerate hands were a huge consolation, I felt miserable and anxious at such dependence, sometimes close to despair.

When Canon Michael first offered to bring me Communion to my bedside, I quickly (and I hope politely) declined. For me, that was a step too far and almost an admission of accepting my complete inability to be part of normal life. In any case, my home did not seem the right place for holy happenings that I have always considered, by their very nature, to be restricted to church buildings and reverent silence except in states of extremis and in other cultures.

A week or so later he offered again and, again, I declined, which, although he said not a word, I sensed his disappointment, causing me to pause for thought. Days passed until, eventually, I changed my mind and we arranged a date although I still felt a certain sense of trepidation.

In the event, my fears were totally unfounded. Michael arrived, as before, gentle and relaxed, his white dog collar brilliant against the black giving a sense of a separate yet accessible being and making the atmosphere feel safe, serene and comfortable. We talked for a while before he reached for his little backpack, a bit like a child's lunch bag, and unzipped it to reveal a number of parcels all carefully separate in bubble wrap.

One by one all was revealed: a little white cloth, a bit creased, a beautiful pottery chalice that could have been a cup for a goose egg, a matching pottery paten, a small wooden cross with two identical wooden mini candlesticks and wax candles fit for a birthday cake plus, of course, the wafers. It felt like a party celebration. All very simple but so special, everything round me disappeared and I was "in Heaven".

The short service was something I will never forget. Next time it might be different as I am now able to get downstairs and there may well be distractions to deal with but I look forward to it with grateful thanks at such a blessing. My prayer is that others may feel moved to take advantage of "that most excellent gift of love" which we are so privileged to be offered in the privacy and comfort of our own homes when getting to Church is not possible and loneliness is a constant companion. It could make all the difference.

26th May 1998

Dear All, Time marches on relentlessly and I seem to be constantly running to stand still. However, at least I am living in my own home and happy despite no cooking facilities (except the microwave and electric kettle), several major water leaks and some lights not working, but these will be sorted out in due course.

The dear little gardens front and back have woken from their resting place under ladders, mortar, concrete and rubble, to give a fine display of one hollyhock, one foxglove, a few cornflowers, quite a lot of granny's bonnets and a host of golden buttercups. I've put in a mature honeysuckle that has idled in a pot since I dug it up from Birmingham and some osteospermums have also survived, as have some beans and sweet peas I saved from seed.

Somehow, I find myself on the flower arranging rota at Church and also the P.C.C. I don't quite know how that happened as I had no intention of being more than a regular attendee at Matins. However, it feels OK and is not very demanding as we are little and local – having said that, we are usually 30+ each week, singing and praising, which would do Charles Wesley's heart good. We have visiting lay preachers and the Rector comes every so often to make us sit up and take notice – it's great! I'm going to Lee Abbey for a weekend with the Parish. They invited me and it seemed a good chance to meet more people and have a look at Lynton again. Watch this space!

9.00 a.m. rapidly approaches and time for our daily hike in the woods with my friend's dog, Arnold.
Love to everyone, JMK

The Journey with Cancer

The road is one of a difficult, constantly changing landscape. From the agonies of initial diagnosis to the relief of being offered treatment, hope and reassurance. From galloping down a race track of abandoned self in perpetual turmoil, to the gentle stroll through spring meadows filled with perfumed relaxation. Over hedges and ditches in a blind rush to an uncertain future and concerns regarding the results of surgery and treatment later. At worst, it is a solitary road (although you are NEVER alone if you can pray). At best surrounded and supported by an army of devoted family and friends – or even just the cat for company – the power of unseen forces, positive thinking and continuing prayers, often from the most unexpected sources, nothing is impossible. Set small targets. Achieve great things. At worst, it is inevitable death and the final destruction of the body shell (but everybody faces that). At best, romance, mystery and eternal life – time to reflect and be thankful, plan and share, healing and reconciliation. The final destination will be an Island of Peace in the Sea of Tranquillity. Heaven

Hip Hip Hooray

Thank you to everyone for the cards, thoughts, enquiries, prayers and acts of kindness over the past weeks since I have been out of action. It is the first time since I gave birth 40 years ago that I have come home from Hospital with a positive addition to my life and I am slowly becoming acquainted with my new hip.

Being stainless steel, and porcelain, it needs care and attention and time to the exclusion of all else, just like a baby, but progress seems elusive and so slow. Clive Orchard suggested I might use this time to write about patience, but I cannot find that word in my vocabulary.

Meantime, the walking sticks and other mechanical aids thoughtfully provided to help mobility and independence are close to becoming weapons of mass destruction as I struggle with the basics. Would you believe that even with the help of a long-handled shoe horn and litter picker there are still ten wrong ways to put your knickers on?

A visit to the supermarket in the wheelchair is another experience I am in no hurry to repeat. Everyone was kind and caring, I had a shopping list and my driver was accomplished and *au fait* with the layout of the store. However, all I saw from my low-slung position trapped behind the basket that stretched far in front, were anonymous kneecaps and impending collisions as we efficiently sped round corners and around displays. Communication with the pilot was difficult and shelves out of reach but, mission accomplished according to the book, I came home exhausted and full of understanding for the less able in that situation.

At home, I have lots of time to reflect and be thankful for things I so often take for granted and have even found that seeking help is not that painful. Slow and deliberate is no bad thing, but will I remember once I am fully mobile again? Only time will tell.

Granny Marnie and Godmother

Tranquillity

The consultant's face was grave as he strode through the door having been hastily summoned to the hospital couch where I was lying, following a series of urgent X-rays. He was compassionate, purposeful and blunt, and although I have no idea what he said, I was left in no doubt that the diagnosis was dire and prospect poor. I felt overwhelming freedom, serenity and peace.

For 25 years I had been a regular blood donor so it was a surprise to be suddenly referred by the Service to my GP who quickly recognised dangerously low haemoglobin levels. I admitted to feeling tired and thought some iron tablets would suffice, but was gently and firmly advised that to ignore the symptoms was 'unwise'. As a nurse, cancer was something I knew a lot about that happened to other people, so it never occurred that I was just as susceptible.

Amidst the busyness of frenetic professional decision-making on this occasion which included alerting my offspring spread far and wide across the world and arranging for somebody to care for the sole occupants left in my house (three cats) there was understandable concern, yet I experienced total tranquillity. No worries!

Immediate, extensive and life-saving surgery quickly followed and, when I came round from the anaesthetic, I was tethered to a cruciform frame, attached to paraphernalia that rendered me helpless but completely pain free, trusting those in charge and at peace with the situation.

A brief moment of indignation at being absolutely dependent for every need was immediately interrupted by the voice of Jesus clearly saying "you could have died – now live!". I would have taken up my bed and walked but was hampered by clumsy attachments and so I relaxed, knowing all was under divine control.

All that happened more than twenty years ago and, although I cannot claim to be always cool, calm and collected, I daily refer to "the author of peace and lover of concord, in knowledge of whom stands our eternal life, and whose service is perfect freedom". He knows me best and gives me space. As Malcolm X wrote "Nobody can be at peace unless he has freedom". Amen to that!

When It's Time to Go

As so often happens in a social gathering of strangers, the subjects ranged far and wide. From the recent Jubilee celebrations to the situation in Syria; education, the extraordinary absence of summer weather and its effect on wildlife, the banking crisis and a whole host of other unrelated topics.

What interested me most was a lively debate around the fact that we are all living so much longer. Well aware that, having passed my three score years and ten, I am already five years into extra time, I later pondered fondly on the fact that my dear little house is well set up with elastic walls and swing doors, where space conveniently expands and contracts, all safe but not impregnable. Sensible precautions like stair rails are in place and a downstairs, walk-in shower and toilet have already proved their worth. My garden is big enough to be fun. A long term solo surviver, having benefitted more than once from the skill of modern surgery, I am determined to stay put at home in the hope that one day I shall wake up dead in my own bed.

Then my fertile imagination and reality take over. Just suppose this happened … or that. Loneliness, depression, immobility, mental confusion, the list goes on. What would I want to happen then? I dread to think of someone sweeping in with a pre-prepared package and taking over. I dread to think that nobody would come at all. I don't want a parent figure, well-meaning and confidently asserting that they know exactly what my needs are. I do want to be consulted and included in the decision-making, however bizarre and unrealistic my views might seem to be. I want respect for my wishes.

It is well reported that the greater the intervention by public services with experts academically qualified and steeped in the misguided notion that one size fits all, the more the community becomes dependent and subservient. Modern technical wizardry can prolong life which is commendable; money can buy time for the elderly in comfortable surroundings and round the clock care which is admirable. Death is natural in the aged but the dying process is not necessarily well managed by our clumsy society in the twenty-first century intent on life at all costs. We could well learn from the culture in parts of rural Africa which I have experienced where they have no such sophisticated systems but compassion abounds in villages among neighbours using the innate skills learnt from forebears and passed on to the next generation.

Whilst I do not want my life to end any time soon, I have left strict instructions that I am not to be resuscitated, but as it seems possible that somebody may well be tempted to jump up and down on my lifeless body, I am tempted to have my chest tattooed with the message: "Please, just let me go in peace". In the meantime, heaven is a place on earth. We all deserve a life worth living and in death, a gentle end. To make it happen, we must not be afraid to speak up for ourselves, making sure we are heard loud and clear, especially by those best able to influence change, wherever they may be.

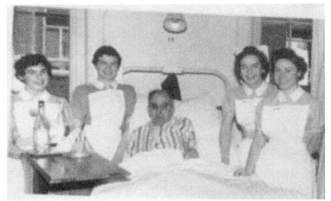

Nurse Jennifer

Kind Thoughts on Dark Days

You will not be surprised to know that I have been thinking about you since our constant routine and contented lives have been rudely disturbed by unexpected happenings and cruel events, not only personal but round the world, over which we have so little control. I could easily fill a book with well-intentioned thoughts and crumbs of comfort, but know that, at this time, officialdom and advice leaves little head room for anything else.

Keep jotting down unrelated notes in a little book - good things and bad, to clear the attics of your mind. Clippings, sayings, happy thoughts and sad, flotsam and jetsam, pressed leaves and flowers, pictures and photos as reminders ... and I promise the sun will shine again from the shadows and most unusual places if we just take time to sit and think, giving thanks for each breath we take and each new day that we see dawning.

Meanwhile, avoid unsolicited press and unguarded comments about anything which gives rise to angst, despair, spite or reprisal. That way the heart ache will ease and heal much more quickly, kind thoughts will filter through the fog and, finally, the wounds will heal, the remaining scars give strength and a reminder that, together with a willing heart, some faith and God's overwhelming gifts, we can survive and move on.

The present is fresh and a precious gift to be used wisely and well. That way we will have 'done our best, to do our duty to God and the Queen' (Brownie promise).

Footcare

This poor little foot has
troublesome toes.
The problem is that
nobody knows.
They're hidden inside
those ill-fitting shoes.
They never feel happy;
they've all got the blues.

How would you feel if
you were stuck in a box
Surrounded completely
by smelly old socks?
So, look after your feet,
you've only got two,
You can't change them
like shoes for ones that
look new!

Adult Life and Dursley

Rubbish

Someone came to my house for the first time and we made polite conversation over a cup of tea and home-made cakes. It was an enjoyable interlude in an otherwise busy week and as she prepared to leave, my visitor, by now quite relaxed, sighed and said "I love your home! It's so full of ..." (there followed a pause) ... "rubbish." Imagine her embarrassment followed by a puzzled expression as I laughed and said how much I appreciated her compliment -- for, to me, that is what it was. She departed, still looking perplexed, but I hope assured that I was not offended.

When I came to Dursley in 1997, I down-sized and de-cluttered my life. No garage to shelter half empty cans of paint, redundant rolls of wall paper, odd lengths of wood, tools and rusty nuts and bolts to mention a few of the things that for years had lain undiscovered but seemed vital to my wellbeing. Not one for excursions into the attic, I determined to surround myself only with things that were useful, easy on the eye, valued for sentimental reasons or absolutely essential to my everyday existence. My bookcase creaks with a jumbled assortment of volumes in no particular order, large, small, fat, thin, old new; travel, poetry, gardening, reference and fiction happily sit side by side to suit any mood. There are notebooks for jottings and papers with interesting tit bits, a jar of pens (rubby out ones for crosswords) highlighters and drawing pencils. Lots of chairs, high chairs, low chairs, folding chairs and easy chairs all with a story to tell. The table is placed in the big picture window overlooking my dear little patch of wonderland that could be called a garden except that everything I plant dies, and Nature does a much better job alone. I do get involved and talk to things that look a bit sad and my wormery delivers lots of nutritious liquid food which I water in now and then. It's not the sort of space that you could open to the public, as some of the flowers are common weeds, but I love them all.

Sometimes I sit and think and write ... or just sit. Sometimes I sew or knit.

Back inside, there are photos of my loved ones departed or far away; ornaments and pictures lovingly hand made by amateur enthusiasts. Binoculars to watch the birds. Houseplants that are beautiful and others past their sell-by date but deserve a chance to survive. I have a "busy cupboard" which is in apple-pie order, and I can put my hand on almost anything, even a pink elephant. There are old fashioned games of Sorry, Scrabble and Snakes'n'ladders and a selection of playing cards which are always in demand if young ones come.

It's true. I am surrounded by things of little monetary value and some age. Call it Rubbish. That's OK. We seem to be galloping down a slippery slope of economic decline, and as I toddle on my own into old age, I am increasingly grateful for the multitude of bits and pieces that make up my home, each and every one conjuring up memories that I know are true, or fancy thoughts that give me pleasure.

My caller was genuine in her honest appraisal and it has given me food for thought.

Thank goodness for charity shops, car boot sales and recycling centres, but there is still far too much going to land fill sites in black plastic sacks which take hundreds of years to disintegrate. Please think about your rubbish before you dump it. You might just save the planet, and if oil runs out and we all have to stay at home, there will still be plenty of things to do that don't need modern technology! It really is up to each and everyone of us to do our bit.

My Ideal

I wonder if an ideal is achievable. I wonder how to quantify it. I wonder how to identify it.

Looking back on an extraordinary lifetime of variety and happiness, I believe I have been pretty close. A wartime childhood, though lacking material possessions was enriched with incidents and personal survival depended a lot on community initiatives, leadership and some good fortune.

My turbulent teenage years were tended by an understanding father, who gently but very firmly reprimanded me on many occasions, and a larger-than-life Godmother who frequently descended, like the gentle rain from heaven, to furnish me with wisdom and confidence well into my adult life.

My nursing career was the fulfilment of a childhood dream, with lots of discipline allowing me to grow and develop in absolute security and satisfaction, to achieve the acknowledgement of hard work and dedication with exams and well-deserved qualifications which I believe I used well.

A happy marriage and busy family life followed and I loved every minute of being a stay-at-home Mum with my husband leading us all through thick and thin. When there were obstacles he simply went ahead to assess situations and minimize major risks, but still demanded our close attention to safety, and a commitment to achieving the best results according to potential. Though I hate swimming and water sports of any kind, I was persuaded to try Scuba diving and when it became obvious that I was not enjoying it, that was the end of the matter. As with many other hazardous pursuits the family did, I was eventually appointed camp follower, which suited me fine.

Though the last 30 years have been less easy, I have few regrets. My faith has afforded me strength to carry on with positive thinking and in the belief that my ideal was as close as possible to realization, given the reality of being human in an imperfect world; I am content.

A recent sudden onset of debilitating ill health has given me new insights and a late onset surprise change of direction with purpose. An opportunity to stop, look and listen. Time to think laterally, quietly, prayerfully and, I hope, gracefully accepting that, though less active and able, there is still a future to be honed, a past to be valued and a present to be used, whatever our age and situation. Maybe not ideal, but hope springs eternal!

I Wonder

It had been a busy week so I was glad to get home to my little house, so warm and welcoming. Mercifully, earlier in the day I had prepared my evening meal so I made a cup of liquorice tea (a recent discovery and highly recommended for reviving flagging spirits), lit the gas under the vegetables to accompany the sausage and mash and sat down to change into my slippers. I gave thanks for my two new hips which, amongst other things, makes reaching my feet so much easier and then began studying the bows that tie my shoelaces.

Who discovered how to do that and, I wonder, when did I learn that particular skill? Of course, there is an official version of the Seven Wonders of the

World, but I thought I would make my own and decided tying bows would be one.

I remember my first Geometry set, beautifully presented in a gold-coloured tin with a fancy label. Inside a protractor and set square, neither of which I ever really understood technically but I loved reciting the theorems with fancy long words like Pythagoras and hypotenuse. There was a ruler and a pencil and a pair of compasses (why a 'pair' when there was only one was a mystery) and I drew endless patterns and circles as if by magic. Great fun and so satisfying.

The bicycle, another on my list of wonders. Thank you, Mr Pedersen of Dursley and all those since who have developed that magnificent machine. Having, painfully, learnt how to ride (I was about ten years old) and been given my first bike, the freedom was exhilarating. By careful management of my pocket money, over time I added a basket, saddle bag and a clip for my tennis racquet or hockey stick and was off. No mobile phone to track my travels, thank goodness, and even when I crashed, I seemed to bounce and was able to cover up the damage.

As a student nurse in the 1950s when the NHS and modern medical machines were in their infancy, we had to rely on our own resources, and I wondered at the way the body, with help and patience and time, can heal itself. I specially recall a chap who worked on the railways and was squashed between two carriages. Seemingly beyond our help, he was strategically placed in a bed by the door and we kept him comfortable, waiting for him to die. Each time I passed by I said a prayer for him. To our great joy, eventually and with no sophisticated equipment, he made a complete recovery. Long afterwards when talking about his weeks in hospital, deeply unconscious, he remembered only experiencing great surges of power which he was sure helped him survive. Nowadays we think nothing of abusing our bodies and expect swift and expensive medical intervention which the country cannot afford. Prayer is on my list, costing nothing except time.

Sitting in my window as I write, I wonder at life itself. The beauty of the winter sky (there *is* glory in the grey!). Trees and shrubs seem almost relieved that they have shed their leaves and can take a rest for a few short weeks, whilst underneath the surface, bulbs are busy growing in the dark and worms are active too, along with all the other microbes without which we could not survive. So much to wonder at!

Are You Sitting Comfortably?

"Once upon a time" … I used to love to hear those words knowing that what followed would be a story full of good news about the baddies losing to the goodies, the Prince finding his Princess, adventure and excitement. Life was simple.

Nowadays all we seem to read about is doom and disaster, not just the floods in India or famine in Africa, but a cyclone in Birmingham and threats of a hosepipe ban and water shortage should make us realise just how fragile our planet is. It is impossible to understand the mindset of the suicide bombers who have wrecked so many lives with their carefully orchestrated terrorist attacks, not just recently in London[1], but elsewhere and over decades.

We hear with great sadness of the sudden death of a great parliamentarian, Robin Cook, and the prolonged final suffering of another charismatic politician, Mo Mowlam, and wonder why? They had no hesitation in speaking out and standing alone against great opposition for their principles. Our country is the poorer for their demise. The immediate and understandable reaction to all these stories is to despair and give up hope, honestly believing there is nothing we can do. We shall be safe at home, not exposed to danger, and if we keep quiet all will be well. This is just what the Devil and his disciples relies on and why evil finds it easy to flourish.

Onward Christian Soldiers, marching as to war with the cross of Jesus going on before ... a wonderful rallying call that we could all rehearse in our hearts and minds to give us the courage to combat our fear.

---

[1] Written in 2005

My family have just celebrated a joyous Golden wedding. The couple's siblings, four sons and their wives and children all gathered for a garden party which, by British tradition, was interrupted by rain. Indoors, we trawled through the photo album and reminisced at length about how things were, are now and will be as we see the next generation carrying the banner of faith into the future. This great party would not have happened without someone's suggesting it, a lot of effort and preparation, co-operation and organisation, but we all felt a great sense of happiness and wellbeing and appreciation of each other at the end of the day.

So if you are sitting comfortably, take a moment to think how things could change around you. Don't be afraid to make the first move, to share thoughts and ideas, however farfetched or difficult they seem to be. Our world is a precious place, our time in it very short and we must make the most of it. Someone once said: *Of all the passions, fear increased lack of judgement most.* May we consider other people at all times and be brave in what we say and do. That journey of a thousand miles needs one step to start it off.

Well, I never ...

At the start of another year, I had plans to dispense with my television set. Understandably, there were raised eyebrows and concern, not least from my adult offspring who, independently and collectively from the four corners of the far-flung planet, decided that the poor old lady really had gone barmy and needed immediate attention. To them, it was like being willingly deprived of what they know as civilised life. Shops shut on a Sunday? Punitive travel restrictions? Lack of running water? YOU CAN'T DO THAT! They made it sound more illegal than unwise and I found their righteous indignation invigorating. At heart still beats that childish, stubborn streak that silently shrieks "OH, YES I CAN!" … ever so slightly tempered by a sensible caution borne of experience.

Parting is such sweet sorrow and I planned for it carefully. Rather like re-homing a faithful pet whose muddy paw prints, shedding hairs and constant demands for attention far outweigh the pleasure of its company, my old TV set deserved a good, useful and happy home for its declining years. A number of approaches were met with various responses, all negative, but eventually a kind soul agreed to "look after it", obviously thinking that I was out of my mind (or soon would be) and before long would want it back.

Months later, and the effects have been amazing. For a start, I feel free. I must admit that I was never a discerning viewer and often regretted wasting time watching what, for me, was moving wallpaper. The vacant space in my sitting room is huge, one small area now occupied by a dear little DAB radio, almost unnoticeable in its neatness, undemanding in its needs, unlimited in its output and inexpensive as well.

I take one newspaper (The Saturday Telegraph suits me fine) and read it steadily through the week when I have time. That and the radio news keeps me abreast of things. Solving crosswords and struggling to master Sudoku occupy my brain cells.

"Sometimes I sits and thinks, and sometimes I just sits" my Granny used to say. She of the wobbly bosom, elastic arms and whiskery chin. Cruelly crippled by arthritis and almost blind, her eyes still sparkled and her infectious zest for life came from her heart, untainted by outside influences. Her faith and love of God was unwavering. I remember her with great affection and reflect on how she would deal with a world of constant change. With space n my mind, uncluttered by visual images beamed into my sitting room instantaneously, mysteriously and miraculously from the outer atmosphere, I, too, sometimes just sits and thinks.

Of course, television is useful and maybe, one day, I shall be grateful for its company. Meanwhile, I can recommend reading *The Forsyte Saga* for a dose of escapism; creating a solo space and listening to the silence – it's called praying or time with God - hearing your neighbours' point of view; tasting life near home and joining in. We all have a part to play, whether old or young, active or not, so let's get together and build a future that is happy and free. God needs our help now.

Friendship

Friendship begins with liking or gratitude – roots that can be pulled up   George Eliot, *Daniel Deronda*
Also … It's about caring and sharing
Trust and integrity
Tolerance and understanding
Minding (but not re-minding)
Honesty and forbearance
Respect for others
Telling the truth however disagreeable
Picking up the pieces and making new beginnings
Having time
Listening and hearing (knowing the difference!)
Comfortable companionship
Forgiveness
Remembering important things
Setting aside incidentals
Not bearing grudges

Friendship is love without his wings George, Lord Byron
Also … It's about taking risks with feelings
Being prepared to negotiate
Gentle persistence
Regular nourishment
Space
Appreciation
Healing time
Encouraging release of bondage of past and future
Using the present
Allowing feelings to take root … slowly

Opportunity for Change

Two of my neighbours fell out big time. Individually, they came to me with almost identical stories which could easily have merged into one as each saw the other as the perpetrator, instigator and guilty party. It was like the beginning of a bush fire in danger of spreading out of control and reminded me of the time when I was cast as a child in the midst of a custody case, and the parents in the play literally pulled me apart in a desperate bid not to lose the battle. The feelings of helplessness, confusion, hurt and the longing for a magic wand of conciliation have never left me. Conflict is so damaging.

Sadly we live in a fragile society where many are born, grow up accumulating unnecessary and costly possessions, indulge in throwaway relationships, muddle through life with no feeling of self-worth and die without any idea that everything we do and say matters and has consequences far beyond ourselves. Einstein remarked that the modern age has perfect means but confused ends. We are richer, better educated, know exactly how things work and break but not how to put them together again. There is a bewildering array of choices. To study or binge drink. To shout at and beat the children as one form of discipline, or smother, spoil and protect them as an alternative. To allow old age to take its natural course or prolong life which has little quality and becomes unaffordable. There are no real sanctions for miscreants and rewards are too easily earned without personal sacrifice or effort. Somebody else will do it, sort it, pay for it. It's all so easy until something goes wrong and there are no reserves. Then chaos reigns.

We moved to Yorkshire form Kent, a long way in 1962, and rented a house on a new estate on the edge of the Haworth Moors. Our incoming caused quite a stir as strangers were rare and we were immediately a focus of attention as if we had landed from Siberia or outer space. When they discovered that our car was very old and battered and that our few belongings were contained in several tea chests and posed no threat as we had far less than they did, they left us severely alone. That winter, our community was isolated by deep snow drifts that reached the tops of hedges and lasted for weeks. Our ancient car, built like a tank with a simple engine that just needed a helping hand with a crank handle to start, left the modern ones standing. We were used to managing water shortages and lack of access to shops and supplies as we had just returned from living in the African bush, so when the gas and electricity supplies failed, we naturally used paraffin lamps and cooking stoves and carried on as normal. Our 'poverty' was a blessing that our neighbours struggled to understand and they were puzzled at how easily we managed with so little and still had enough to share.

Misunderstandings and disagreements seldom happen by chance, but are the end result of a chain of events for which we are all responsible. An equable society will only happen when we acknowledge that we all have spots and pimples, amazing strengths and palpable weaknesses, irritating habits and fascinating interests that can add up to a priceless collateral which, if freely shared and graciously accepted, is beneficial. In what promises to be a time of austerity, there is an opportunity for change and an even greater challenge to overcome all sorts of differences by being sensitive to others but first we need to believe that having less does not mean being poor and being rich does not necessarily equate with happiness and contentment.

For the record, I invited my neighbours to my house for a cup of tea. I am optimistic that the wounds are beginning to heal, but fear the scar may not disappear completely any time soon. We'll just keep trying.

A Collector's Piece

"Now, *that* might be very *you-sif-full*" my four-year-old daughter was absolutely adamant, though I was not convinced that a sopping wet, battered sailor's hat could conceivably add anything to our lives. Each and every day, we would walk along the village street to leave my other two children, aged five and seven years, at school before taking the narrow, short, well-worn footpath to the beach.

Sometimes, the wind howled and the waves crashed on the shore making any conversation next to impossible, in which case we would find a sheltered hidey-hole and just sit and watch in awe and wonder, hypnotized by the force of nature and excited by what we might later find washed up when the tide ebbed.

At other times, the sea made gentle shushing sounds on the shingle and the sky was reflected in the still surfaces of the puddles of various shapes and sizes scattered amongst the shiny rocks. Princess Pool was much bigger, seeming like an ocean to a small child with endless imagination and a capacity to be quite content anywhere in, on or near water – something she has maintained into her adult life, having swum, surfed, dived and kayaked in places round the world from the icy wastes of the Arctic and Alaska to the Caribbean, Africa and Australia.

Whatever the weather, we would stay until it was time to persuade my reluctant child that we should go home so that we could have lunch together whilst *Listen with Mother* was on the radio. To this day, she blames *The Archers* which was broadcast immediately before, for unnecessarily interrupting her blissful existence. (*Listen with Mother* does not exist in her memory) En route, beachcombing was, of course, imperative and her collection of "you-sif-full" articles continued to grow and develop as she gradually learnt to be discerning and found that things that are rotting or dead are best left behind.

Forty years on and there is a seaman's wooden chest under my stairs, undisturbed and crammed with treasure more precious than a pirate's stash of gold bullion. I do hope that one day she will open it and happily ponder on those days of careless rapture. It is always possible, of course, that all she'll find is the disintegrated, unrecognizable remains, but everything has a story to tell as any archivist will say, and I know she will be up for that.

I'm Glad

It all began as a very normal day. I opened the back door and a gentle breeze stirred the leaves of the scented geranium whilst wispy white clouds waited high up in the azure sky like athletes on a starting block. As usual after breakfast I met my friend and her dog for our regular daily exercise - an hour's ramble up in the woods and over the hills, exchanging gossip, swapping ideas and sharing news, views and concerns. We have known each other since school days and recently, in retirement, become neighbours - a situation realised only after protracted poring over maps and estate agents' offerings and, bearing in mind that we lived hundreds of miles apart, an amazing piece of good fortune.

On this particular day, conversation inevitably turned to the pressing need to harvest the red currants in her garden, the blackcurrants already finished, strawberries and raspberries gasping their last and the tree fruits still in their infancy. Suitably clad in sun hats and shorts we set about the tedious task and three hours later I returned home across the road triumphant with six pounds of fruit. Wimbledon had finished - no great surprises as Sampras stayed supreme and Becker and Graf retired to even richer pastures - so with no excuse to while away the hours watching tennis I tackled the time-consuming chore of preparing the fruit. Jam requires meticulous pruning so I settled for jelly which needs much less effort - or so I thought. With pans full of beautifully-coloured boiling liquid, I realised I had no jelly bags to strain it through. After considering, and discarding, the idea of some muslin nappies which even sterilised did not seem suitable - I hit on the idea of triangular bandages from the first aid box. Perfect, except they were vaguely tainted with TCP and needed sewing into shape.

Nothing daunted - yet - I fetched the sewing machine from its dusty perch in the pantry only to find the needle missing. Eventually I located a replacement (sensibly stored by the threads) and swiftly sewed the seams. So far, so good, except you need somewhere to hang the bags of boiled jelly juice ... for hours whilst they drip.

In Granny's kitchen I remember acres of space and hundreds of hooks strategically placed. Modern buildings have no such things, so I hastily rigged up a Heath Robinson contraption incorporating the plate rack and plastic tubs. In need of string, I nipped out to the garden shed, finding all sorts of distractions on the way... a slug, some dead heading, a few weeds ... An hour slipped by before I returned to the kitchen to set up and complete the original task ... then, it was evening ... another day gone. Totally exhausting, absolutely absorbing and satisfying in the extreme. Thank you, Lord, for all your blessings and especially being able to enjoy retirement.

The Garden

As a child, my daily walk to school took me through Grove Park in Weston-super-Mare, sadly no longer the beautiful place I remember. I used to read on a stone: "You are nearer God's heart in a garden, than anywhere else on earth". Who could possibly argue with that, when each day the colours and smells were governed by so many amazing things? Which way the wind was blowing. Cloud cover. Sunshine and rainfall. Temperature. Time of day or season of the year.

On the lower level there was the green grass, sometimes verdant and covered in daisies, sometimes dry and worn or wet and soggy, but always inviting us to do cartwheels of joy on the way. Further along we climbed a slope, canopied in summer shade with dappled shadows, or spooky with bare branches swaying in the winter wind.

Then we scrunched through the fallen leaves, gathering conkers and acorns. God was never far away.

Many years later in Africa, not content with the jungle that surrounded our little house, I scratched at the bare earth and planted tiny seeds, watered them and tended them carefully, with no result, and resigned myself to being a failure. In retrospect, of course, I should have realised things don't always grow to human order.

Back in England living by the sea, I struggled again and even a move to the country did not help as the soil was heavy clay. I did not have the strength to dig it over or the funds to get help. We moved again and my next-door neighbour grew all sorts of vegetables and flowers. Over the years we worked hard in tandem with the seasons, learning from success and dealing with failure, thankful for our fellowship and God's guiding hand.

It would be good to say that I never struggled after that, but I did. Always trying to grow the best, getting rid of weeds, slugs and snails with chemical mixes of any kind. Spending money on ridiculous exotics and fancy blooms which usually expired without trace or outgrew and smothered the rest. I did not stop to think.

This year has been so different. For various reasons,

I have left my beloved garden to its own devices. Absolutely no chemicals (only a bit of powder to ground the flying ants, I felt was justified). Prolonged absence from home early in the year meant very little tidying up so all manner of seeds have sowed themselves. My bean plants look like lace curtains where every type of munching maggot has had a feast. (There are still enough beans just for me each day.) I have so many different flowers that I have had to buy a book to identify them, and the butterflies and bees have had a ball. The geraniums that spent the winter neglected in the spare room, have enjoyed being outside and bloomed non-stop. It's a pity that there are very few birds to eat the slugs and snails, and despite a little pond, no frogs. Even my compost heap does not seem to boast any slow worms to help my cause. But as I sit and enjoy the beauty of all that has happened, I feel total wonder, and know that if we can just "let go, and let God", He will never let us down.

2000

When the Heart Stops Beating

At the age of six, towards the end of the second world war, I had already planned my future career as a nurse. For a short while my cherished father was stationed at Locking, the local RAF base, and whenever they had a few hours to spare would come home bringing with him colleagues who lived further afield. They obligingly became injured war heroes needing my special care and, when my mother wasn't looking, I happily ripped up precious bed sheets to make bandages!

The whole of my school career was irrelevant as I dreamed of looking after lepers in Africa or galloping round on a horse in the Australian outback and being an essential member of the Flying Doctor Service. To fill the yawning gap, I spent most of my education time doing sport and drama and all other lessons lazily gazing out of the classroom window. The moment I was sixteen I left, with no real exam results, and began work in a Child Health Centre - the start of five years concentrated learning on a diet of study with just enough time left over to run a Christian Union Group and play competitive tennis. It was a surprise to everyone that I had a brain after all.

I qualified as an SRN and celebrated my twenty-first birthday in 1958 and was persuaded by family friends to go on a blind date to a Formal Ball, a totally new experience that changed my life. I fell in love that night.

After three years courting, during which I gained diplomas working in Casualty, Plastic Surgery and TB nursing, we married and went to live in the African Bush where my husband was a diamond prospector known as "Big White Jumbo". I was "His Missis" and ripped up his shirts for bandages when our first aid kit ran out. It was an exciting time of great adventure.

Back in England again, the swinging sixties gave way to the seventies and we were already the envy of those whose marriages were faltering. Our home, with three children and a menagerie of assorted pets and pastimes, was a haven for all and sundry. An ever-open door, elastic walls, plenty of floor space for sleeping bags and always enough food to go round. The ultimate Good Life of security and happiness.

We had just celebrated our twenty sixth wedding anniversary when my world fell apart as my adored husband suddenly disappeared without trace. I knew he was stressed and anxious but his job as Director of Security in the Northern Ireland Prison Service was extremely demanding and I assumed that the best way to be supportive was to keep the home fires burning just as my Mum had done so admirably during the war.

In due time I discovered that I had been traded in for a pregnant mistress ... a story as old as time. Tragically, that resulted in the birth of a profoundly handicapped child and it was no comfort to me that the Bible says: "I am a jealous God and visit the sins of the fathers on the children". With our grown-up family dotted across the world, I felt I had no future and attempted suicide which failed because the only hose I had did not fit over the car exhaust.

It took a very long time, but with great help and support, I rebuilt my life and career but, sadly, despite my best endeavours could not save our marriage. He stubbornly remained at large from all our family and friends for more than twenty years until our son, on the verge of emigrating to Australia, managed to trace and see him. I had naturally hoped for reconciliation too and hearing that he was terminally ill, I offered to care for him but it was not to be. He died, rapidly overcome by a series of vicious cancers leaving everyone who knew and loved him battered, bewildered and wondering what caused him to choose the wilderness and was there another way? We will never know for sure, at least not this side of eternity, but this is what we do:-

Put one foot forward and then the other
Lift our eyes to the snarl and smile of the world once more

Decisions and Choices

Several years ago, I decided to give away my TV set and since then have relished the space it left in my sitting room and the spare time I had to fill with doing all sorts of other things. This year, I chose to borrow one, just for the Wimbledon fortnight. My friends were secretly (and not so secretly) speculating that it would become a permanent feature once more and I did wonder if, having given up driving, I must just succumb.

I more or less hibernated, and was fascinated by the little red button that allowed unlimited choice of matches, avoiding irritating grunting Slavs to be replaced by captivating doubles duels. British interest in the singles was uplifting and the men's semi-final will long be remembered. Everything reached another level when Murray and Djokovic reached the final.

On the same afternoon another attraction was to take place locally in St James' church where, according to the advertisements, "music pupils ranging in age from six to *burble burble*, grade ½ to 8, burgeoning skills and a variety of instruments" were giving an informal end of year concert.

Without a manual or government decree on this occasion, I was free to consider choices and make my own decision which was a refreshing change when so much of our lives seem to be driven by political legislation and profit margins. I watched the first set of the match and was satisfied. Then I walked to Church for the concert which turned out to be the most joyful and inspirational occasion. Apparently informal, as promised, but it could have happened only as the result of a lot of practice, organisation, harmonious team-work, enthusiasm and support from a large number of people.

During the interval there was a happy hum as artistes and audience mingled, feasting on afternoon tea and delicious cakes plus strawberries and cream, of course. There were so many stars on and off stage but special mention should be made of Caroline Marrow who, having had singing lessons as a Christmas present, sang a solo to a small sea of familiar faces which earned resounding applause and great praise.

Lynne James was the teacher, arranger, conductor, organiser and beaming focus of a unique occasion, unstintingly supported by absolutely everyone. Long may she reign!   Incidentally, the TV has been returned and the space will be filled … with a music centre.

July 2013

Change of Life

It all began when I was 21 and given a surprise course of twelve driving lessons. I was not best pleased; not in the least bit interested in cars and far too busy with what little spare time I had free to be bothered with it.   My friends and I lived in the Nurses' Home. Off-duty, we played tennis and went dancing. There were plenty of trains and buses if we felt the urge to venture further than the Greasy Spoon café not far from the hospital which had a juke box and was always burgeoning with interesting people.

So, I went to the School of Motoring to cash in the tokens. To my great disappointment, this was not an option, despite my pleas of poverty and total unsuitability to be eventually let loose in sole charge of some lethal cumbersome weapon. After much soul searching, mostly alone with my totally unbiased best friend, Jesus (all my earthly confidants thought I was mad to give up such a prize!), I booked one lesson and duly met my instructor.

He was a big, bold Yorkshireman who had obviously been carefully briefed and despite my determination not to get involved, I found myself sitting in the driving seat and gingerly moving the car down the road, carefully keeping close to the kerb, even round a lay-by. We had words and, at the end of a tortuous hour, he told me to come back next day. Like a lamb to the slaughter, I went.

After five tricky sessions, he booked me in for a test which I thought rather rash, but imagined that he had already given up on me, so I would fail and the sooner we got it over the better. Meanwhile, his teaching was firm and one thing he made me do over and over again was a hill start on a bend at a junction with the main road. It became obvious that until I was confident, he would make me keep doing it. Years later, I went back to see if it was really as bad as I remember. It was. In fact, the hill seemed steeper and the bend more curvy. I passed my test first time and this lovely, big bear of a man positively beamed.

It was a very long time before I drove again and then it was only out of necessity when we lived in the country where public transport was non-existent.

Our cars were a succession of vintage vehicles with strange arrangements of pedals and pumps and erratic handling, so my early tuition in mastering machines in challenging situations was invaluable. Years later I treated myself to a brand-new model with power steering and, arriving home the first day, misjudged the garden gateway and crashed into the wall. Nothing prepared me for that.

Recently, my dear little motor has spent a lot of time idle so I sold it, ending a 55-year career of almost incident-free motoring. A huge sense of freedom has left me with precious time to live life differently. Trains are a wonderful, stress-free way to travel long distances, if only someone would run a user-friendly bus service that serves the station …

Home

Henry James called it *a great good place*. Ideally an oasis of calm where the body can relax with time for the mind to rest and be thankful. It is often connected to childhood, a whiff of happiness from long ago: a plate, a picture, a smell or taste linked to the place where it all began. *We wove a web in childhood, a web of sunny air* wrote Charlotte Brontë. There is nothing wrong in wanting to recapture what is perceived as endless days of cloudless skies, gradually expanding horizons and tempting space.

My husband was a man for whom there were no obstacles that could not be overcome – just challenges to be met and managed. Home was always wherever we happened to be, however, temporary the location. He converted a baker's battered, very old delivery van to transport and accommodate us, our three young children and a menagerie of animals on endless journeys and adventures. We purposely left the firm's logo *Mother's Pride* printed large on the side. Black and white photos of school holidays and picnics, parked up in some open space, often swathed in blankets, always surrounded by bats, balls and bags of food are reminders and proof of the fun we had, even though things did not always go exactly as expected.

There were no computers and mobile phones the size of matchboxes were still a figment of the inventor's imagination, but ghetto blasters like small suitcases and huge fluffy muffs for ear phones were sometimes allowed as a treat in the absence of what we grown-ups considered more suitable pursuits for our spirited offspring. As teenagers, they readily followed where their father led, as he encouraged them to develop skills in increasingly daring pursuits. Being far too timid to join them parachuting, gliding, diving and motor cycling, I was quite content to be a stay-at-home Mum, ready to welcome them back, sometimes bruised and disappointed, often wet and weary, but always starving hungry and eager to get out and about to try again.

One bitterly cold winter, the sitting room of our London home was devoted to boat building and when Spring came and the finished article was ready to be presented to an unsuspecting world, the dinghy was too big to go through the door, so windows were duly removed for the launch. Bemused neighbours watched as it was loaded aboard our battered old car for the long drive to Cornwall, leading to their lifelong love of being in, on or under the sea.

Now, those young people are middle-aged and scattered round the world. Their homes (one ocean-side and one in the mountains, both in Australia, the other in rural Scotland) are varied and interesting meccas, all using modern technology whilst, maybe even subconsciously embracing the principles of simple pleasures that shaped their early lives, a time which is already history as the world has rapidly and irrevocably changed.

It is a pleasure and a blessing to me to be able to visit and see them all happy and leading full lives. I am glad to be over the horizon of worry and ambition with a freedom to ponder and enjoy, without envy or regret, the collective results of what constitutes their homes, and to know, deep down, that there is a little bit of me in each one. As the early 20th century poet Khalil Galbraith wrote in *The Prophet: Parents are the bows from which our children, as arrows, are sent out.* I say Amen to that!

Family Matters

My 8-year-old daughter was heavily into history so we visited museums at every opportunity, though my limited knowledge was constantly stretched. At the end of a very long day in the British Museum, London, Frankie insisted we could not go home until we had seen the Elgin Marbles. A kindly attendant duly directed us along miles of corridors and up endless stairs. As we entered the gallery, I expressed doubt that we were in the right place as all I could see were massive pillars and enormous statues.

"Oh Mummy!" sighed my child in despair that only an uninhibited offspring can express with unsolicited love. "I bet you were looking for bowls of little balls!"

How right she was!

Time to Stand and Stare

As a family we moved from the country to inner city London. Our children were then ten, nine and eight years old and delighted that our new home was on a very busy crossroads, with dozens of big red buses continuously passing by and a nearby Tube station ripe for investigating. I was paralysed by fear of the unknown, confused by the relentless noise and, when alone, I just stood at the window and stared, pretending that it was TV out there and could be switched off.

I was forced to venture forth to see them safely across the road to school, but it felt like a motorway and, to begin with, I stood stock still and stared vacantly at the steady stream of threatening vehicles. They soon got the hang of the situation as children so often do, and before long I was being propelled through the air as their combined chorus yelled above the clamour: *Ready Mum, NOW!*

I can honestly say there was never the expected screech of brakes or angry tooting, so I quickly learnt to rely on their good judgment and trusted their road sense. Sadly, I am still rubbish without the guidance of lights, zebras or pelicans.

One day we were given a book on serendipity in London – a dear little volume that easily fitted into a coat pocket and contained vast quantities of exciting and trivial information about the city. Every weekend, all together, we sallied forth with sandwiches and high hopes to discover new things. From carvings of dolphins on the seats along the Victoria Embankment to statues of long forgotten inventors, pioneers, explorers and benefactors, to say nothing of wandering round museums, exhibitions and art galleries, where the world slowed down and instead of chewing petrol fumes, we leisurely breathed the fresh air of new knowledge. Sometimes is it good to make time to stop and stare.

A Stitch in Time

It took 25 years but eventually my knitting became a bedspread that always reminds me of my perseverance, enterprise, skill and dedication. The pattern is intricate with knobs and spaces, blocks and lacy bits. The material is white dishcloth cotton, so hard wearing, warm and endlessly washable. The whole, achieved with just two needles and my hands, produced an heirloom, totally devoid of any artificial input from computers or modern machinery and technology. Ageless, unique and simply enduring, in everyday use, not hidden away protected from daylight or burglars. Of no monetary value, it encompasses a lot of effort and spans an ocean of memories that will last for ever. I am proud of that.

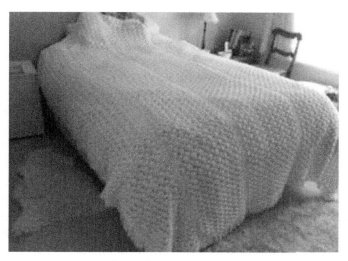

Me and Mechanical Devices

I have always avoided close and personal relationships with anything that did not breathe or grow in the ground. It's true that as a little girl I tried hard to persuade my beloved Bristol Granny (the one with untethered and wobbly bosom, facial whiskers that tickled when she cuddled me and sparkling eyes that always made me giggle) that she should have an electric iron when she was adamant that the flat iron she heated on the fire could not be bettered and, as she continued her practice of spitting on it to accurately gauge the required temperature, I was forever persuaded that modern inventions need to be treated with caution. In fact, I have only recently and reluctantly replaced my 55-year-old electric iron and am not enamoured of the new one with all its fancy bits and pieces.

Learning to drive was sheer necessity when living in the country with three small children in the 1960s and no public transport. The trouble was that our cars were always old and needed cranking, repairing and replacing at regular intervals and were far happier with a fearless male driver than a woman and umpteen children. My husband could drive anywhere without incident, whereas I was often saddled far form civilisation, no means of raising help and with the prospect of a long walk home. So much easier to walk in the first place. I well remember in the 1980s having my first new car and found the power steering so effective I ended up parked on a stone wall!

About twenty years ago, I embraced the inevitable and accepted a 'pay as you go' mobile phone which I am still learning to use, am in no hurry to update and am more than happy that it is considered archaic and a conversation piece (most recently featured on Facebook). Whilst I admit it is a useful tool, it is not essential to my daily wellbeing. The whole population was at one time wedded to fax machines, soon followed by affordable PCs and I found my far-flung family trying to persuade me that my life would be greatly enhanced if I embraced these modern conveniences. It made me tearful and anxious and, I felt in danger of being abandoned by society as everything went automatic, immediate and impersonal, but was demanding attention and mental energy I was not prepared to expend.

I did, eventually, get a computer which was a virtual elephant in the room, totally overwhelming. Despite lessons on basics which meant I could use emails and write articles, nothing else made sense and I felt manipulated by moral blackmail and almost a failure, but I had neither the will nor the confidence to stand firm and declare independence. After years of trading uncomfortably, I finally took the plunge and got rid of my TV and computer in 2007, feeling as though I had freed myself from torture. There were raised eyebrows but no major earthquakes and life went on for several years until it was suggested by my daughter in Australia that on my next visit, I could buy an iPad en route.

Having no idea what this meant, I resisted the urge to ignore the idea and promised to have a look at the airport where I found a very nice, kind, caring salesman who patiently explained how it worked. He told me how his Mum was like me and had been totally won over by this new phenomenon and, after much careful thought, I bought one, spending the rest of my long journey regretting my decision. However, when my daughter cheerfully offered to add it to her vast collection of gizmos and gadgets, I figured that my little package could quietly fit into my luggage and life if I took things sensibly and slowly.

So, it has proved. It has taken a while, but it is not the merciless master I was in awe of. It is not the monster of modern invention I abhorred. It is simply a machine ready to respond to my demands. Even when I lose my way, nothing really bad happens and there is usually a way back. Only recently I was stumped when it 'froze' and none of my learned friends or professionals could work out why. It was not a life-threatening situation and could wait, so I left it alone for a day. Then, after a few prayers, I came across some mighty small print in an obscure corner that suggested in refreshingly simple terms pressing two little buttons simultaneously, and it worked! True I had to then remember how to get back into the system, but I did it all by myself. Such joy! To all others of my generation of 80-year-olds I say, we can do it ... our way!

Busy Doing Nothing

I woke up early. The grey skies and cold east wind belied the fact that it was mid-summer. It was Sunday but our Morning Service starts at 11.30 and, between us, we had set up the Church the night before, so there was no immediate rush.

I enjoyed a leisurely breakfast in my dressing gown and slippers, sitting in the picture window overlooking my cottage garden where, despite the gloom and doom about diminishing numbers, bees were a-buzzing in droves. They didn't seem to mind that recent gales had flattened the honeysuckle arch and most of the pretty flowers they visited were common weeds to the connoisseur as nothing posh survives in my plant jungle. Sparrows and blackbirds, harassed by huge hungry babies quite able but too lazy to feed themselves, needed seed but the bird table was bare. So, without bothering to change, I pottered outside.

Half an hour later, I had filled the feeders, done some dead heading, noted quantities of leaves reduced to lace curtains by voracious appetites, enjoyed the various colours and scents and was surprised by a shrub which had been unceremoniously dumped, now showing determination to survive despite the indignity of being considered rubbish.

Back inside and mindful of my Granny's fervent declaration that *he who on the Sabbath pares the horn, better by far had ne'er been born*, I settled for a swift scrub with the nail brush and some polish in an attempt to rescue my manicure *before* doing the washing up and tidying the kitchen. Not very clever. As I put the milk bottles outside the front door, a neighbour passed by and stopped for a chat, and then I saw the runner bean plants bursting out of their little pots and desperate for more space. The sun was peeping round big fluffy clouds so, still in my nightie, and without gloves or proper tools, I soon settled them happily in a growbag already in place next to the south facing wall.

The clock, meantime, had relentlessly moved on and important choices had to be made if I was to be quickly transformed in time to get to Church to light the candles, ring the bell and welcome all-comers in my role as meeter and greeter, suitably clad and refreshed.   Over many years of practice, I have perfected the art of quick changes – from various uniforms to sports gear as a teenager; from working Mum to dinner hostess as a wife; and from leader of the pack to tail-end Charlie, rounding up our offspring and their countless friends in a variety of pursuits before producing filling meals as if by magic … to mention one or two! I confess, I often made do with a lick and a promise in place of a shower and make-over. There was never enough time.

Later that day, back home once more, nourished by Holy Communion and fellowship, I pondered on the wonders of the world that happen by the Grace of God and which we, so often, take for granted. Seasons come and go, of course there are changes, hidden surprises, desperate disappointments, anticipation and purpose, diversity, determination, stress and deep sadness. That's life. However, there is so much to be gained by sitting still, seeing and thinking and giving thanks, even if it means writing *I love you* in the dust and having nothing to show for being busy doing nothing. The mental miles travelled and the peace of an idle mind, without mechanical noise, in company or alone, for however long it takes, is worth cultivating and can be more healing than a pot full of pills. My beloved granny (her of the wobbly bosoms, twinkly eyes, whiskery chin and elastic arms) used to say: *sometimes I sits and thinks. Sometimes I just sits.* Amen to that!

Precious Possession

They were very special. A present from my beloved father as I left home at 17 years old to take the first steps in my chosen career as a student nurse: a pair of scissors. In the early 1950s as much a tool for the trade as a scythe to a farmer or thread to a cobbler. A most important part of my uniform and jealously guarded. They were so essential that I had them chained to my belt. That way I could not lose them and certainly never let them go.

Much later, they were part of my luggage, indispensable in the African bush and one of the very few things that escaped a devastating fire. Back home, with young children, they were used for everything from first aid to cutting paper for make-do-and-mend, almost the only thing that had a place and woe betide those who used them and forgot to put them back. I did not let go.

Time marched on. We moved house umpteen times and the children had all left home. One day my scissors were nowhere to be found. I was heartbroken and spent many fruitless and wasted hours hunting for them with absolutely no idea when or where they were last seen. I would not let go.

Then, my son the scallywag, who sometimes showed promising signs of maturing into a sensible young man, asked if this was a life-threatening matter. Of course not! I then gave thanks for my father's precious gift which had been such an important part of my life for so long and let go.

A few weeks passed. Alone and with a little spare time, I scanned the bookshelf for something to read with my coffee and took down a rather dusty copy of *Pilgrim's Progress*. To my amazement, there they were, like the light at the end of the tunnel. A miracle! I am so glad I let go ... and let God ...

Deserted Wife

I'm cold and frightened
My nerves are on the outside
No one will help him or me
No one CAN help, can they?
I must have help
I must talk to him
I'm tired of living
Everybody talks
Nobody tells me what I should do
Nobody knows what it's like
I'm tired – why does he hate me?
I can manage but only if I talk to him

Perpetual Motion

After two years pre-student experience in clinics and hospitals and three years general training, I was proud of my new role. Twenty-one years old, fully qualified, distinct uniform to match the status, lots of welcome responsibility and a much sought-after post as a Staff Nurse on the Women's Surgical where Sister ran a tight but happy ward. Life stretched out ahead of me, full of promise, no more studying, just limitless fun and fulfilment. I had arrived!

In retrospect I fear I was guilty of youthful arrogance as I vividly recall being told gently, but very firmly, that my learning had only just begun. Since then, half a century has disappeared into history with an almost relentless momentum of new beginnings and fresh challenges that always seems to end up just short of that far horizon. Now, at 70, I feel almost grown up.

Last year, for the first time since they were teenagers, my three adult offspring were all together with me for a weekend reunion and once more, I thought I had arrived. Suddenly the years between condensed comfortably into contentment, and once more life stretched ahead, full of different promises. All of them, and me too, have experienced the joys of wedded bliss followed by the unbearable heartbreak of divorce. The inevitable scars are carefully filed under 'E' for experience which each of us uses differently, sometimes wisely but not always too well. We have learnt to listen to well-meant advice, but do not necessarily act on it. We are joyful for independent living and the luxury of security in our relationship that allows exploration and testing new ideas. A bit like bouncing on a trampoline that is surrounded by safety netting just in case you misjudge your landing. We are a family, after all, made with the same ingredients, but butter, eggs and flour don't always turn out as cakes.

So, what next? My son is joining his sister in Australia; one daughter lives happily in rural Scotland and next summer my youngest daughter and I are booked on a small, suitably equipped ice-breaker to circumnavigate Spitzbergen. She will seakayak while I watch, from a safe distance, for polar bears and ice bergs.   I am still learning, reaching for that far horizon and having fun too.

Unexpected Outcomes

About a year ago I was faced with a BIG life-changing decision: whether or not to have milk delivered to my door.

So much consider – more expensive, of course. Supposing I had too much and it went sour? Then I would make a milk pudding or find my Granny's recipe for scones which is lurking on a dusty shelf in my busy cupboard along with other long forgotten treasures.   More seriously, what if I ran out and had none for a cup of tea? Then black coffee would be fine and the corner shop is only a totter away.

The milk is farmed locally and *treated not depleted*; the cows graze out in the fields. It took a ridiculously long time to come to a decision but I finally took the plunge and signed up, half expecting failure at the first hurdle. I need not have worried as the service has been faultless.

What has been surprising is the unexpected pleasure as, three times a week, I open my front door at breakfast time and find my cool bag filled with goodies that have arrived, as if by magic. Like a Christmas stocking, it gives me such child-like joy.

Very occasionally, in the wee small hours, I may hear the gentle clink of glass bottles and the purr of an engine, but nothing much and I have never seen the phantom deliverer to whom I am so grateful. Even in the snow and ice, getting up our hill seemed to pose no threat.

If I am helping one person keep a job and, in so doing, it means that one farmer and one cow are peopling our countryside a little longer, I am happy to pay for that. It makes the milk taste even better and starts the day with a smile.

This week I sold my car, have given up driving and, thanks to the local computer shop and support from a young friend, I have updated my little laptop to a grown-up machine that is simple and understanding. One day maybe I shall buy a TV so that I can watch lots of sport. Life is filled with changes that can seem daunting, but I am ploughing a steady furrow through my seventies as a solo survivor, having fun, and surprising my family along the way. It will soon be time to pack my bags for Australia again. Meanwhile the garden needs attention …

Sharing and Caring

I was born by the seaside and grew up surrounded by countryside, so it was a huge shock when later, married with three children under 11 years old, we went to live in inner city London – Brixton, in fact. Our house – rented as part of my husband's job – was dwarfed by tower blocks and commercial premises on a main road at a busy crossroads.

Before we had time to surface from the packing cases on the very first day, there was a major car crash outside my front door. All I could do was dial 999, but it was more frightening to hear the voice at the other end of the phone say: "Scotland Yard, can I help you?"

"Oh no! I don't need YOU! It's only a major road accident with lots of people injured!".

"Well, Madam," said the kindly sergeant, "we do deal with other things beside rape, pillage, murder and mayhem."

That was a surprise, but in no time ambulances, police and the fire brigade arrived and everything was under control as all of us played a part, mindful of each other but obedient to the co-ordinator. Little did I know that that was the start of many years of my liaison with the emergency services around the junction. I soon learned what I could cope with, with local help, and when we needed to call in the experts. Before all this I'd given policemen a wide berth believing that I need not be involved as I was not a law breaker, nor lost or lonely – in fact, I was independent and quite able to manage without them – thank you very much!

It reminds me of my relationship with Jesus. By getting to know Him it is possible to become a team, ready and able, any time, to tackle anything. Even miracles are possible. He is the perfect co-ordinator, always at the end of a prayer call. All we need to do is ask for help. He will respond and if we trust in Him and believe in ourselves, all will be well.

I Love the Place Where I Live

Dursley is a small market town with a huge, proud historical and agricultural heritage. From Tufa rock quarrying to rope-making and weaving; from woollen mills to Lister-Petter engines and Mawdsley machines. The birthplace of Edwin Budding, inventor of the lawn mower and once the home of Pederson, whose remarkable ingenuity produced the safety bicycle.

Nestling in a sheltered valley of rolling hills and peaceful countryside at the southern end of the Cotswold Way, convenient but not too near a meeting of the motorways, visitors coming by car or on foot are greeted by stunning views as they drive down the wooded hills and winding roads that land them in the flat bottom of town. Award-winning ale awaits the thirsty at The Old Spot and numerous cafés serve a variety of refreshments whilst little shops sell all sorts of goodies you did not know you needed.

The last sixty years have seen change and development here, as everywhere else, with manufacturing declining and businesses disappearing to be replaced by housing for commuters and families alongside an ageing population of long-term residents. Existing societies and organisations flourish and new ones begin. At a first attempt in 2011, the town's entry won a Silver Gilt Award in the Britain in Bloom competition.

In 1996, I was living in Birmingham, nearing retirement and spent much spare time exploring the three counties – Hereford, Gloucester and Worcester (all areas new to me) before, quite by chance, finding and falling in love with a dear little cottage built in 1914, lovingly neglected and hiding in a back street in Dursley. Only after I had lived here for ten years did I discover that in 1840, my great-granny, then aged three months, was living in the Union Workhouse long since demolished, that used to stand at the end of the road where I now happily live. She and her family were destitute victims of the collapsing economy. How history comes to life! How fortunate I am!

A Winter's Tale

It was 8 a.m. on a bitterly cold, dark, drab December Monday morning as we gathered at St James to catch the coach for the start of our day of Pilgrimage. The driver was a jolly fellow and we made good time down the M4 with a stop en route for refreshments and convenience. As we neared Guildford, Sofia Denno, Skye's beautiful daughter, provided a spectacular diversion by being overcome by travel sickness. Miraculously medi wipes and mini mops appeared from numerous survival kits so order was quickly and quietly restored. Once in town, mother and child disappeared into the local departmental store for fresh clothes and all was well again.

Meanwhile, down a very narrow street, we had a warm welcome at St Mary's Church. Small, plain and rather too well white-washed, but with an amazing history dating back to William the Conqueror, it boasts a story that one wall had been knocked down on the orders of the Prince Regent when the carriage he was in got stuck in the alley.

Rev. Janet presided over Holy Communion for us which, needless, to say, was very special. Then we were free for a while, but the pouring rain put paid to sightseeing for most people so shopping was a good alternative with Christmas only six days away. Four of us, with immediate priority of food, followed our leader, Austin Meares, on a fast lap in search of a little eatery he remembered from his youth. Sadly, it had changed beyond all recognition in forty years and was almost as cold, dark and draughty as outside, but after much hilarious debate, we stayed put.

Mid-afternoon, in the gathering gloom, we continued our way to the Wintershall Nativity play. The coach driver skilfully navigated us down tiny country lanes in bitch black, through narrow gateways and found our final parking place, but we still had a long uphill stagger on rough, muddy ground. There were flaming torches along the way, maybe more hazardous than help, but nobody said pilgrimage is a picnic.

The first part of the production was outside and Mary on the donkey with Joseph came from one direction while the shepherds and their live sheep appeared from another, battling the elements for real. Clever stage lighting and microphones were discreet but effective. We were thankful to move into a huge barn for Act 2 and the rest of the story which started with a tableau of the Holy Family and, in thirteen scenes, covered everything from the Annunciation to Epiphany and the Three Kings, a splendid Archangel suspended on high, the flight into Egypt, Herod and eventually the victory over Satan as he was dramatically driven into Hell. The triumph of the Angels drew it all to a close. Back on the coach there was a buzz, a mixture of contented awe and wonder and gentle snoring. A day to remember with special thanks to Rev. Janet for, without her, we would not have been there.

I Remember

We loved and laughed when first we met,
Then fate stepped in between.
I kept the precious ring you bought,
Tho' you were nowhere to be seen.

As time went by, I loved you more –
I never heard a word –
Until one day that phone call came –
"I'm home" – the only words I heard.

We met again and talked a lot,
So much had changed, so much the same,
We loved and laughed and promised more
A summer passed and autumn came.

Our wedding was a lovely day
With friends from far and wide.
They came to share our happiness
And when we left them all, I cried.

Within three years we'd celebrate
Our tiny house bulged at the seams.
Three babes plus dog and an *au pair* too,
(the train down the lane was driven by steam!).

Now those babes have grown and flown,
Our home is shared by cats and fish.
The days are lonely, nights are cold,
If only I could wish one wish.

I wouldn't ask to win the Pools,
Or jet set to the sun.
I'd ask for you to come to me
My husband, my beloved one.

No job or house or fortune
No money clothes or car
Is half the worth of loving someone
Whose other half you feel you are.

Faith, Hope, Trust and Thanksgiving

It seemed a good idea at the time. We were in the Lake District on our way to Scotland. We studied the map carefully, choosing an 'A' road which was relatively straight and going North and set off in good faith. It soon became apparent, as those who have travelled the Kirkstone Pass will know, that not all 'A' roads are two lanes with a decent surface. As we drove, the road got steeper and the visibility got worse until we were shrouded in mist, with a rock face on one side and a sheer drop on the other. There was no turning back – even when we saw a huge orange shape looming out of the gloom. We pulled in close to the side and with great skill the other driver squeezed safely by. We were so thankful.

Later, as we reached the summit, and without warning, we were confronted by a white coach which appeared out of the fog so suddenly there was no escape. There was a loud bang as our car slid into a small ditch but, to our surprise, kept moving, albeit very bumpily and on the level. A little further on we came to a standstill, safe in a passing place but in a large puddle. The coach had long since gone.

We were so thankful to find the only damage was a puncture and, in good faith, reached for the mobile phone to get help. No signal. The silence was deafening but, as the odd vehicle passed by, the car was rocked by spray from the torrent of water and we were surprisingly raised by cheer. We were not alone. I ventured outside and managed to flag down some passing headlights only to find the occupants were also visitors to the area but Good Samaritans too. We had no idea of our exact location but they assured us they would get help somehow. We could only wait and hope.

Eventually our earthly saviour came. He was thankful to find us in one piece as there were no landmarks to pin point us. By the time we had unloaded the boot to get to the spare tyre we were very wet and cold, but full of joy and thanks that even in desperate situations there are solutions if we are prepared to seek help, trust in other people and be thankful for the experience. The Lord surely works in wonderful ways.

Consider Other People

My three children were born in three years and because of their father's profession, we moved house frequently. It was great fun, but took a lot of organisation. We adopted a motto: *Consider other people* which has stood us in good stead to this day. From minor misdemeanours like being rude, shouting, dropping litter or not sharing toys, to more serious issues like running in front of a car without looking which my youngest daughter did one day. She was not badly hurt but the driver was very shocked, of course, and she got the message.

Each week was named for one of them and, when it was their turn, that person had all the privileges, like sitting in the front seat of the car, licking the cooking bowl clean, choosing a favourite meal and so on, BUT, that week they were expected to help round the house, make sure the animals were clean and fed and to be available to run errands if required. They quickly realised that having rights also meant honouring responsibilities. Of course, it wasn't all plain sailing, but it was a sound base camp to launch ourselves from. Our house was always full of their friends and, as teenagers, they hosted a weekly motor bike club at home when no other venue was available. The neighbours were very understanding and the members had strict guidelines about noise and going home times. Despite their unconventional attire and geeky ways, they were valued as people and responded accordingly with care of our property and respect for others. It worked well.

All of a sudden, or so it seemed, I am Granny (proud and prejudiced, of course) to my son's daughter. Her parents divorced many years ago and, despite the geographical distance and other difficulties, she and I have maintained a close and loving relationship. An only child, now sixteen years old, she is busy flexing her fledgling wings in a world that is so different from the one that I and my children grew up in, but she too uses *consider other people* as a benchmark. There are huge uncertainties for us all, but being a teenager has always been fraught. Smoking, drinking, sex and drugs hold no fear, it seems. Gangs gather, make a lot of noise, leave rubbish behind and appear threatening so people are, understandably reluctant to get involved. The trouble is, like the neglected levees which exacerbated the recent floods in New Orleans, if we fail to address society's shortcomings, matters will get worse. We are rich, sometimes greedy, often thoughtless and selfish, poor in spirit and short-sighted. By walking on the other side, we can appear to be offhand and uncaring. The breach becomes wider. Recently, Rev. Ian Gardner gave a powerful sermon on *Who am I?* and *Who do you say I am?* which gave us all food for thought. Pause for a moment to remember all the identities you have had in life so far, then, how other people see you now.

The other day I met an 85-year-old man looking sad and shrivelled, like a withered tree. We got chatting and he positively blossomed as he told me about his experiences in the RAF during the war. He was shot down and taken prisoner by the Germans. As he talked, he took on a new identity. When we parted, we both felt so much richer in spirit. He felt valued and I was entranced.

Now let us think of the young people who gather in the Churchyard. Instead of 'What on earth are they doing here?' try 'What are they doing here on earth?' How can we begin to understand? Can we make them feel welcome and wanted instead of alienated and apart? It is not easy, but neither is it impossible. Prayer and positive thinking seem a good place to start. May God be our guide.

Please Remember

For more than 30 years and through many house moves, one thing remained constant in our house: a plaque hanging in the bathroom. A beautifully illustrated poem by Mabel Lucy Attwell: *Please remember, don't forget.* It bore the ravages of time, constant exposure to heat and steam and looked very tatty. An impending visit by my daughter from Australia fired my enthusiasm to spruce things up and it was gathered up in one of the many bags that went to the charity shop.

Frankie duly arrived and was heartbroken to find a vital part of her childhood had vanished to be replaced by a modern version, detail identical but in total absolutely sterile. I didn't sleep that night and next day we passed the shop to find the missing treasure had pride of place in the window, still looking tatty but beaming like a beacon on a dark day. Maybe not a miracle, but an answer to my prayers and now back at home on the wall, it is a daily reminder of my blessings.

PLEASE REMEMBER — DON'T FORGET —
NEVER LEAVE THE BATH ROOM WET. —
NOR LEAVE THE SOAP STILL IN THE WATER.
THAT'S A THING WE NEVER OUGHT'ER.
NOR LEAVE THE TOWELS ABOUT THE FLOOR,
NOR KEEP THE BATH AN HOUR OR MORE
WHEN OTHER FOLKS ARE WANTING ONE —
PLEASE DON'T FORGET — IT ISN'T DONE

Mabel Lucie Atwell Illustration

So, as we embark on another New Year with temptations to make resolutions, to change things, to throw out the old, discard possessions that are no longer new, all in the name of progress, perhaps it is time to stop and think. We live in a world that is moving so fast it is almost out of control and certainly in danger of implosion. Each one of us can make a difference – by caring and sharing, by listening and, above all, hearing others' concerns and opinions, taking them into consideration and acting accordingly. We can all learn and contribute, from the cradle to the grave and beyond. For sin to thrive, it simply needs good people to do nothing. Let's all make an effort to make our wonderful world as good as we can for everyone.

What is one of the most expensive things that you've ever bought?

To me, money has always had a plethora of interesting facets causing hugely diverse reactions, rarely really positive. Too much and it causes personal greed and public envy; too little and the poverty trap ensnares the humblest person to the point of despair. I like the idea of bartering which, of itself, has no intrinsic value, but used wisely and well and with goodwill, makes for a richer community.

For a while, about twenty years ago in our town, we had LETS – Local Exchange Trading Scheme – which worked so well that by offering my domestic skills of cooking, sewing, knitting, child-minding, in fact anything that revolved round my numerous local commitments, I earned enough points to have my house re-wired. Expensive in time and effort, but no money involved, just total satisfaction all round.

My husband was a sort of petrolhead so we were always surrounded by a variety of vehicles, large, small, two wheels or four and, once, a three-wheeler, all in varying states of repair but amazingly roadworthy when he drove them. I seemed less fortunate and once, on a particularly wet and windy winter night, fed up with trying desperately, alone, to nurse one of them home down dark, narrow country lanes, abandoned it in a field and felt safer and more in control completing my final five miles on foot. Needless to say, he retrieved it without recourse of tools or any aid. It was then, and with the benefit of a bequest from my Granny's Will, that I decided to take unilateral action and get something I liked, that was more reliable, just for me.

I don't recall any lengthy consultation, but it was not long before we had visited the legendary Morgan works and I had ordered myself a bespoke hand-built, two-seater, dark blue sports car. This was the 1960s and, compared to today's complicated, computerised cars, was very basic but complete with leather strap over the bonnet this was the epitome of expensive grand motoring, albeit totally unsuitable as family transport, considering we had three young children. Nevertheless, I was a very happy Mummy and they were happy too.

The waiting list was long but I didn't mind. Better to journey than arrive springs to mind, as the promised date for delivery nine months later came and went with no sign of it coming off the production line any time soon. I felt let down, cancelled the order and, soon afterwards, we surprisingly bought a cottage in Cornwall instead. That really was the biggest expense with the most non-monetary lifetime benefits for a huge host of people. I have no regrets, but boundless happy memories and am eternally grateful for 'our creation, preservation and all the blessings of this life' and am still an ardent advocate of bartering.

My Birthday

All of a sudden it crept up on me. May has always been my favourite month with so much promise of new beginnings and looking forward to long, hot days of endless sunshine and free time with no school to worry about. Lilac and lily-of-the valley and laburnum, cow parsley, clematis and cranesbill all competing to be the best of nature's burgeoning bouquets as spring flowers, past their best, gracefully give way to a younger generation.

This May has been special and, dare I say it, one of the best as I celebrated my 80th birthday.

When the family first addressed it two years ago and gently enquired if I had anything in mind to mark the occasion, I was keen to go to Cuba and the seeds began to take root. Excited at the idea of realising yet another dream that had forever seemed impossibly remote, rather risky and extremely exotic, it was, at last within reach. However, fate had other ideas and, in the meantime my health wings have been clipped so that long-haul trips are not straightforward or advisable. We had to think again.

When our children were small, we were fortunate enough to buy and live in a very old and rather dilapidated Coastguard's cottage in Cornwall which we owned for 20 years before circumstances forced a heart-breaking sale. Now it is an upmarket self-catering holiday apartment which we decided to rent for a week. Fortuitously, my birthday fell on a

Sunday, so invited guests from far and wide, gathered on Saturday night and stayed, with others finding local lodgings or came for day visits.

My presents included all the food and drink for main meals and I happily baked tea time treats and rich fruit cake which all travelled well. The weather was kind so whilst the able-bodied took long beach walks, others braved the narrow lanes by car or motor bike, to enjoy places like the Eden Project and Land's End or revisited hazardous haunts on exposed cliffs they enjoyed thirty years ago. For my part, I was happy sitting in the garden with the sea at the front gate and gentle ventures on the shore collecting pretty stones and smelling the sea air.

On the last day, when everyone else except my daughters and I had gone home, there was a change in the weather as though it were planned. The wind blew a hooley, the waves crashed and the sand shushed, just to remind us of why the cottage was there in the first place, and the old Coastguards whose lives were devoted to dealing with shipwrecks on the rocky coast.   Indoors we were cosy, warm and thankful for so many new memories to add to the old ones.   Our family and friends are scattered, but this week has brought us all together in a very special way and I am thankful for all that! Roll on next year!

Boat coming in to Downderry
our family home 1969-87

Thoughts and Meditations

Nature's Gift

As I sat, having my breakfast at the table overlooking my garden, my attention was drawn to a bush drenched by overnight rain and I noticed a single drop of water that, catching the sunlight, twinkled like a star. If I moved my head just a nod one way or the other it disappeared, so, for a few quiet moments, I sat mesmerised and tried to indelibly imprint that picture in my brain.

Then the breeze stirred gently, some little birds bounced on the branches, the whole bush shivered uncontrollably and broke out in a rash of shimmering sequins. Just as quickly, the show was over and then I noticed a robin sitting solo on the overhead wires, singing away and daring any challenges to his territory. Silhouetted against the pale blue sky an aerial combat between a David and Goliath of the bird world seemed to be more about agility and skill than warfare and winning.

The soft sun moved silently on, peering into dark corners, catching cobwebs and highlighting countless colours of the plants and flowers, from the deepest brown that is nearly black, to the palest lemon. The wooden gate, the stone pillars, slate tiles, cast iron furniture, plastic pipes and pots, street lights and TV paraphernalia are all reminders of how human kind shapes and changes the natural world. Progress is inevitable, a balance of interests necessary and caution essential, lest we end up in dire need for the sake of greed and instant gratification. It is a delicate situation needing urgent attention by each one of us before we lose, for ever, the goose that laid the golden egg.

Doing Christianity

Anyone can BE a Christian ... you just say "I am what I am" and providing you keep a low profile, break no laws and show up at Church now and then, the chances are nobody will challenge you. To DO Christianity is a whole different thing. You must be prepared to stand up and be counted, to be jostled and teased and made to feel uncomfortable and still believe that you are never alone.

We lived at the "top end" of a housing estate attached to the Prison where my husband was the Governor and our son, Neil, was about 9 years old. He often came home with bruises and torn clothes and it was many months before I discovered (from another parent) that he was target of bigger and older children who thought he was a goody-goody. At the same time, he was a devoted member of the Cub Scouts who met in a leaking hut with no facilities, but their Leaders had foresight and determination which they instilled in the Pack. Fund raising was a hard graft. However, newspapers were a lucrative source of revenue if somebody would go round the houses and collect them, tie them in bundles and store them, but as everyone knows they are bulky and very heavy. Nothing daunted, Neil persuaded us to vacate the garage for storage, asked people to keep their old papers separate from the rest of the rubbish (recycling as we know it had not been invented) borrowed his sister's doll's pram and each week did his rounds. He was hurt that he was scoffed at and puzzled when adults in particular, pointed out that he was not likely to see the new Scout Hut built as it would take forever. That was true, but he persevered until we moved away and lost touch with the project.

Thirty years on, we have been back and found that eventually it did come to fruition. There is nothing to say how or by whom or when ... just a magnificent building achieved by small feats of endurance from a lot of folk and perhaps a lot from a few ... but isn't that a testimony to the fact that no matter how hard the road and impossible the task, we should take heart and carry on if not for ourselves, for others.

Turning Things Upside-down

Let's face it, we have all been guilty of causing chaos hunting for something in a hurry, or asking the Lord to take care of things when we run out of steam, expecting solutions NOW!

My friend and I were about to embark on a long car journey and I was surprised that, before we set off, she dedicated the day to God and gave thanks for our safe arrival! That seemed odd to me!

Some weeks later I mislaid my car keys as I was about to leave the house when something made me stop panicking and, as I sat quietly, I found myself saying 'Thank you' for all sorts of things. My keys appeared and all was well.

Another day I was due to drive the M25 in atrocious winter weather and at rush hour. I engaged Jesus as my co-pilot before setting out. There was a lot of traffic but no hold-ups or accidents, the spray seemed more like lace curtains than an ice blanket, there were very few daunting continental container lorries on the way and my car refused to do more than the speed limit. (Like a lot of us I do want to go fast!) The result was, it took the same time as on a fine day and I arrived feeling totally relaxed.

Maybe next time you feel tempted to ask for something try saying *Thank you* first: it could make all the difference.

Let's Go

Where are we heading in the middle of 2018 as temperatures rise and tempers fray? It's hard to imagine Jesus wearing a face mask and fully protective clothing, spending precious time and resources protecting himself from the unseen enemy whilst exposing the majority to fear of the unknown.

Imagine having to don wet suits and breathing apparatus with heavy cylinders before diving through murky waters in pitch-dark narrow tunnels at great personal risk, giving hope to the seemingly hopeless and inspiring others to believe in the impossible. What lessons have we learned from recent headline news apart from the fact that miracles can happen, and when even the greatest efforts don't result in a World Cup coming home, or the most modern medicine cannot save lives, brave leadership and committed team work makes a whole lot of difference.

We should all be caring, or, if limited to four walls for whatever reason, secure in our faith, still somehow sharing the daily challenges faced by those so badly served by masters sitting in high places, insulated from poverty and unreachable. We should be walking alongside the lost and lonely whose friends are alcohol and drugs, and those who hunger for help but find it impossible to ask.

Why do Churches have walls and heavy doors that are frequently locked for fear of vandals? What are we doing about it? Do we really care? Do we feel helpless in the face of adversity? Are we just idle?

The least we can do is pray, wherever we are whenever we can. Just treat Jesus like a friend whose ear is always open. He hears but may not respond immediately or in a way that is obvious or to our satisfaction, but He knows best. If we make the effort to reach out into the abyss where the impossible abides, just maybe we will dull that invisible pain that beleaguers others and perhaps cobbles us too and, who knows, gain insight ourselves, give incentive to others, sow seeds of hope and reap a harvest of deep thankfulness.

We are not all given to be leaders, or contenders or trained to take life-threatening risks, but the wheels need constant oiling by those who gently and quietly persevere unseen, unrecognized and often publicly unrewarded, but devote time and energy to all manner of jobs and services, groups and teams.

I treasure the memory of the day, 75 years ago when I solemnly made my Brownie promise "to do my best to do my duty to God and the Queen ..." that has stood me in good stead ever since and I commend it to everyone as an anchor in any situation. All together now, let's go.

The Taxing Journey to Bethlehem

In those days Caesar Augustus issued a decree that a census should be taken of the entire Roman world so everyone went to their home town to register. Joseph had to go to from Nazareth in Galilee to Bethlehem as he belonged to the house and line of David. He was with Mary who was pledged to marry him, and pregnant. They would have had company for the dangerous journey and the most direct route was southward across the Jezreel Valley, then up along the rounded hills and weathered peaks where the Samaritans harvested olives, figs and grapes on the sunny slopes, and grew wheat and barley in the sheltered valleys.

On the way, they would have passed many of the sites of stories from the Old Testament and the eighty miles would have taken about a week, their journey necessary so that they could pay their poll tax which went directly to Rome. But there were also food taxes, land taxes, transport taxes, purchase taxes and customs duties.

Even then, with a population of only 500, Bethlehem was a busy place, situated near the main road from Gaza to Hebron and if the inn, or caravanserai was full, local people would have lost no time in offering hospitality to passing strangers. It is more than likely, however, that Joseph, himself, would have sought a quiet place for Mary to rest and give birth, away from the raucous crowd of camel traders and mule trains.

Bethlehem is 2500 feet above sea level and nights would have been chilly at that time of year, so the animals were brought under cover for food and warmth. The manger where eventually Jesus was gently laid was possibly a stone feeding trough filled with fresh straw bedding. Renaissance painters can be forgiven for romanticising the scene but, whatever the truth, it is certain that Joseph did his very best to ensure the safety and comfort of Mother and Child during their arduous, long and dusty trek, so soon followed by labour and birth.

The more I think about Joseph, the more I warm to him. Plucked from obscurity, wounded by wagging tongues about the scandal of pregnancy before marriage, the future was scary and he could, understandably have been overwhelmed. Nevertheless, this gentle country man, so much in love with the young and vulnerable Mary, seems to have shouldered huge burdens with quiet fortitude and dignity, qualities which are, sadly, airbrushed out of popular historical narrative. A man for all seasons, blessed with a wife whose courage and devotion, too, proved to be indomitable, theirs seemed to be a match made in heaven but their suffering unimaginable.

How spineless we are in the 21st century complaining about comparatively paltry inconveniences and claiming poverty when we have so many riches that money cannot buy. We should think on these things, and be thankful.

What is Your Best Relationship Advice?

Amoebae change shape, move freely, extend and contract, can be overwhelming and parasitic, but also have an amazing ability to survive challenges. They are much like relationships, except that amoebae are harmless.

From the experience of great age, I can muse and pontificate on all sorts of things, propose solutions and share experiences in the vain hope of being heard and helpful. However, relationships advice is far from straightforward and comes a long way down my list of offerings. Each couple, family group, neighbourhood, organisation, school, company, government and country has its own size and shape embracing a dynamic collection of personalities with opinions that defy constancy, even in routine, and people who may not welcome unsolicited advice.

For the benefit of this exercise, I suggest that any relationship is best placed in an equilateral triangle for the comfort of parameters with a place at the tip for someone to take overall responsibility and the rest of the shape gradually growing mathematically, available for thoughtful, individual input, allowing for the passage of time and changes in society. Even a twosome benefits from a leader, then with respect and understanding, within a safe environment, freedom is the gift in which to develop and grow families, organisations and ethics.

Maintaining any relationship is a joint exercise but must be mutual. Once those boundaries are compromised and threaten wellbeing, difficult choices must be made, whether individual or corporate. Whether to challenge or compromise, leave or stay or just do nothing. Whatever the outcome, bear no grudges that eat away like cancer, have no regrets that are like anchors holding fast in deep and choppy seas whilst preventing fresh landings and new starts. Parting is such sweet sorrow but temporary, and scars heal over in time. Death of spirit and soul by any means is self-destruction and everyone has a life that deserves to be valued. Being alone does not equate to being lonely. As Woody Allen wrote: *relationships need to move on or die.*

Happy Thoughts and Sweet Dreams

The trouble with dreams is they have a habit of taking on a life of their own. I dream of a secret garden, a magical place where the sun always shines, the birds always sing and there is ample time to sit and savour silence. *You are nearer God's heart in a garden than anywhere else on earth* is something I learnt as a little girl at my beloved Granny's knee (her with the wobbly bosom, elastic arms, sparkling eyes, infectious giggle and whiskers that gently tickled my face when she cuddled me). In the acres of my dreams, colours would be soft and subtle and scents heady and lingering to attract butterflies and bees. Even weeds would be welcome as long as they were pretty and well behaved.

A woodland area would boast a carpet of bluebells, primroses and snowdrops and, in due season, lots of wild anemones and garlic and a majestic spreading horse chestnut tree to supply shiny brown conkers for competitions. The cottage garden would be a riot of hollyhocks, delphiniums, foxgloves and cow parsley, stocks and rudbeckia, clumps of succeeding colour from spring to autumn with mature shrubs and hedges for shelter form the salt spray as my garden would be by the sea. Lovely frothy fronds of pink tamarisk waving in the breeze, quite happy in a howling gale, plus yellow azalea, berried pyracantha, delicately perfumed honeysuckle and ivy scrambling up and over the dry-stone wall, providing welcome nesting sites for a variety of birds. A terrace of riven Cotswold slabs with gaps left for camomile, alyssum, marigolds, camomile and calendula to seed themselves each year, would have a rustic bench. Interesting pots and planters would be scattered and moved around according to my whims and fancies, but no tiresome, labour intensive, awkward and thirsty hanging baskets.

The formal herb garden, strategically sited by the back door, would be a geometric marvel of squares and triangles, planted up with parsley and thyme, basil and marjoram, sage and rosemary, lovage and fennel, each area separated by a neat, low, self-clipping box hedge. Separate pots would be planted up with different mints, including apple, ginger, pineapple and spearmint, and a ball-shaped bay tree would stand proud by the pretty porch smothered in a deliciously scented rose with window sills laden with scarlet pelargoniums. Altogether a veritable medicine and cosmetic resource with lavender for the linen cupboard and lingerie drawers an absolute must. A small pond is home to frogs and lily pads.

The kitchen garden would grow salads and vegetables and there would be a south-facing wall for luscious sun-ripened espaliered tropical fruit. A straight path leading to a small wooden gate makes easy access to the adjacent orchard where sheep graze under the apple, pear and plum trees, all yielding abundant produce for jams and jellies, tarts and pies to fill the pantry when winter storms prevail.

Camouflaged by the dappled shade is a green door where only I can go. A secret, silent place of tranquillity and peace with a roundhouse made from wattle and daub topped by a thatched roof reminds me of the time when I lived, simply, many years ago in an African village. Furnished only with a day bed and cushions, a sanctuary where mosquitos and bitey things are banned, time is infinite and dreams can come true. Just supposing you stumble across this special place, please tread softly and maintain the peace or the spell will be broken.

Let's Talk

It is not simply a question of economics or ethics, escape or ease, but all about personal opinion, and longs for the opportunity of an open forum, free from fear of favour and so often denied a platform for reasonable debate.

Euthanasia – that big, bad word that has no heart. That spells spine-chilling split-second decisions or long considered, secret aims seeking personal release without retribution. It is also about caring enough to allow life to end, comfortable and painless, ensured that all will be well.

During my lifetime I have had numerous experiences of pioneering surgical and medical intervention that have restored me to perfect health and I am eternally grateful. As a ward sister in a cottage hospital run by GPs in the 1970s in London, I had the privilege of moving mountains to rehabilitate more than one ancient body anxious to get home to the cat and canary, as well as respecting the wishes of those who felt their useful and fulfilling time on earth had come to an end and there was much more living to be done "on the other side".

Most recently, I have been mercilessly tethered to unbearable pain and loss of mobility, surrounded by loving family and friends, but often close to despair at the enormous gaps in access to basic professional support when it is needed most. There are such huge, and often unnecessary demands on the NHS, always expensive and often wasteful, leading to stress at source for both patient and practitioner when time and resources run out for those in greatest need.   Life is for living and we all have a responsibility to make it the best we can for ourselves and each other (sharing matters of concern would be a good place to start).   Learning about simple illnesses and how to deal with minor accidents, without clogging up surgeries and casualty departments would make a difference and could save more than one life and avoid a lot of misery.

In addition, honest and frank discussions about difficult issues like death, inevitable as it is, is freely available to all, requiring no more than a willingness to talk and listen with an open mind. My much-loved mother-in-law announced that she was quite happy to be dead, but minded very much about the way she died. It was the perfect opportunity to hear her hopes and fears. Sadly, hers was not a happy ending, due to circumstances beyond our control, which is regrettable. There is no single solution but society as a whole must do better for our ageing population and not leave it to politicians and pontificators.

Just Think About It

It's a fact of life that, in many places of work, staff wear labels, unobtrusive and easy to read if you so wish. As a customer, I quite like the fact that the person behind the counter, the nurse, bank clerk, bus driver, ticket collector or whoever, has a name and takes on an individual identity rather than being just another anonymous body in a huge organisation or place that may be unfamiliar to me. A name is a useful reference.

So I find it difficult to understand why there is so much comment when I choose to wear a badge in Church. It is plain and simple with just my Christian name written in black type on a white background, indicating I hope that I am part of the place and a point of contact. Curiosity I can cope with, but not disdain and ridicule and assumptions that I have delusions of grandeur. I know strangers are met at the door by smiling meeters and greeters but they can disappear into the congregation as the service begins and may not be easily identified again at the end. If the celebrant has a long queue waiting and staying for coffee is not an option through shyness or time constraints, anyone with a badge could be a lifesaver to a shy visitor.

It is tragic that those who have been Church attenders for any length of time, forget what it is like to be an outsider looking for a way in. Holy huddles are comfort zones with everyone facing inwards like a team focussing on winning an important game. Nothing wrong with that, but we must remember that we owe a duty of care, particularly in these times of increasing social concern, to those for whom the Church is a tempting place of refuge but where the rules of engagement are not easily accessible. If, by wearing a badge, I can help one person to feel they belong, I will happily endure being misunderstood myself.

Winter Wise

I used to loathe the winter – those long, dark nights and dreary days when it felt as if you were suffocating in an ever-decreasing space of no hope. Then a very dear, respected, adored and ancient friend said: "think of it THIS way - The darkness we so often dread can be seen as a symbol of rest and recuperation". How wise.

It took a long time but eventually I heeded her words. Come autumn, I took stock, put away summer clothes and tucked up the garden, not with mounting misery but with a real sense of purpose in giving them all a rest. At the same time other outfits and ornaments came into their own. A library list ensured plenty to read, completion of a 1,000 piece jigsaw was satisfying and even my old-fashioned radio showed no signs of age but brought lots of happy memories flooding back. I wrote long letters to family and friends who seemed to find it amusing that I am not about to swap my pen for a fax or any other machine.

When I got tired of doing things. I shut my eyes, dreamed and schemed, plotted and planned for a future that may never happen, but at least I've given it time and thought.

All of a sudden, the clocks have gone forward and spring is on the way. I shall miss my thinking time and those long, dark nights and must remember that as we see the resurrection of the earth, so we must make time to rest and be thankful. Every day is a day the Lord has made.

All Change

It seems that this time of year – the season of mists and mellow fruitfulness – has more upheavals, fresh starts and new beginnings than any other. Tiny tots take their first steps on the long road of formal education whilst elder siblings find the giant leap to secondary school scary, but are soon confident in their new surroundings. **They have all been prepared**.

Days get shorter and the shadows lengthen, so we swap summer clothes for sweatshirts, put the barbeque to bed and harvest the garden. Chimneys are swept and the central heating serviced ready for the winter. **We are making preparation**.

In April, I was in Boscastle, recently devastated by flash floods[2] and the main road in Scotland I drove

---

[2] This was written in 2004

along in August has disappeared under a landslide. Further afield, my friends in Florida have lost their home to hurricanes Frances and Charley. Whilst there were warnings, nothing prepared any of these people for the upset and disruption that overtook their lives and the months of rebuilding they must face. Now the world is reeling in the aftermath of the Russian massacre, and not for the first time, man's inhumanity to man is beyond belief. **No chance to prepare, negotiate or compromise.**

So, where is God in all this turmoil? It is a good question. I believe He is right there in the middle, hurt, angry, disappointed and anxious. He does not let bad things happen, but allows us the privilege of free will. Along with rights, we have responsibilities and must exercise them wisely. **We should prepare.**

Global warming is caused by our disregard for our environment, overuse of motor cars, water and other resources. Deadly diseases are spread by lack of basic hygiene. Demand for instant gratification makes us selfish and extremists flourish in a climate of greed. It is a very slippery slope which we ignore at our peril.

What can we do? We can change by being more sensitive to every situation. Find out why, for example, the Chechnyans did what they did and pray for their redemption. What causes flash floods and hurricanes and pray that more understanding will help reduce risks. Close to home, be more caring and sharing in the street and neighbourhood. Pray for insight and discernment. Have courage to act on issues you feel strongly about, however simple or futile. (I am fed up with footballers spitting and am planning a campaign.)   Prayer is a powerful tool, requiring nothing except focus and attention. If you are prepared to give it a go, it could change the world and wouldn't that please God?

Mini Meditation

I often "sits and thinks" or even "just sits" and the recent spell of winter weather (I refuse to call it bad) has given me plenty of excuse to do that.

I remember the 1960s when I was a busy housewife and mother of three small children, finding every waking minute of my life accounted for. The local GP was a friend to all and offered unsolicited advice as he met people on his rounds, so it was no surprise that, one day, he suggested I would be wise to try to build ten minutes free time into my daily routine to help me enjoy life a little more. I thought I was happy and contented with my lot, but respected his opinion enough to give it some consideration.

Everybody of course knew that old folk (especially men) had forty winks after lunch, but the notion of mini meditation for all and sundry had not been invented and, if it had, would have been dismissed as rather quaint. How times and fashions change!

So my suggestion is that we should all make provision for some inaction every day. For a few minutes, escape the slavery of time, take off your shoes, (you are not going anywhere) switch off or simply ignore the phone (make yourself unavailable). Sit comfortably with a straight back on a chair (no slumping on the sofa and going to sleep) rest your hands with palms face upwards (no fidgeting with rings and fingers) close your eyes and put your mind in neutral. With regular practice I promise it is possible to be completely refreshed, with a clear head, and energy and enthusiasm that, previously, would have seemed an unlikely outcome in so short a time.

Going fast does not equate to achieving more. Reflection is viewing the past rationally. It leads to a more efficient way forward and leaves room for new ideas which all helps relieve stress. Try it. Ignore the jibes. Just sit there and see what happens.

Who Cares?

Suddenly it is September and all over the country families are experiencing mini tornados, earthquakes and volcanic eruptions which have nothing to do with the weather but everything to do with the end of the summer and the beginning of the new academic year.

Tiny tots are getting ready to take their first steps on the school ladder and, "miggles" brace themselves to become "bigs" as they move from Infants to Juniors. Without doubt, the greatest transition is for those who have been important in their Primary school and must face the huge jump to the Secondary scene. Much larger buildings, many more teachers and subjects, further to travel and all so scary. Some are set to move further away to embark on independent living.

Amazingly, they nearly all take it in their stride and soon become self-assured mini adults. Beneath that veneer, however, lurks huge uncertainty and mixed emotions that can manifest themselves in thoughtless behaviour and non-co-operation which leave all grown ups gasping for breath fearful for the future. We must not fail them.

My teenage years were painfully turbulent. I had absolutely no interest in school and lived for the weekends and holidays when roller skating on Weston prom was my favourite forbidden pastime. My poor mother got cross and despaired at what she saw as rampant hooliganism, but thankfully my father remained steadfast whilst expressing disappointment that I chose to be rebellious. I left home at 17 years of age and missed him dreadfully, but he kept faith with me, and I responded by behaving responsibly in return for his trust and understanding. I remember him with gratitude and love.

I also remember the first time that, as parents, we stayed out much later than planned and received a severe scolding from our teenage children who were at home worried to death. We all learnt a salutary lesson that night.

Sadly, not everyone is blessed with good parents and a supportive family. Today it would be so easy to give up in despair as our world seems to be in meltdown and facts are often sacrificed for a good story that sells papers, but we all have responsibilities, no matter how old (or young) and regardless of status or gender.

Age is just a number but experience spans the generations so that wisdom can be found in the adolescent and may not necessarily visit the old. Two-way communication is so important and we must bravely address difficult issues if we are to continue to survive unbowed. "Please explain ..." is often a good way to open a conversation to tackle a thorny subject such as a difference of opinion, litter or loud music. Adults can be guilty of that too. We are not beyond reproach.

What, Where, How and Why?

When I was growing up, post-Christmas celebrations always included a visit to the pantomime at Bristol Hippodrome. Wartime restrictions made such outings very special. The vast auditorium stretched up to heaven with twinkling silver stars, glittering gold furnishings and posh plush seats in front of a velvet curtain which hid the huge stage. The story of the show was always a familiar fairy tale; we joined in (sometimes even went on the stage), booed and hissed and cheered and sang and really believed that our valiant efforts made a vital difference to the "baddies" being beaten and everything being "happy ever after". And then I grew up.

This week I went to another pantomime. No big theatre with lavish decoration but a modest Church Hall in an outer London city suburb. The very small stage stuck out amongst the rows of plastic chairs, packed so close together there was hardly room to breathe. The orchestra numbered five, separated from the audience by a painted line and all playing at least two instruments each. The story was "Jungle Book" and we had such fun booing the "baddies" and hissing at the snake, but best of all cheering Tarzan (played by the Vicar), a slim fellow whose muscles had to be augmented with plastic and whose knobbly knees would have won any contest. There were lots of children dressed in balaclavas, brown t-shirts and tights who made magnificent monkeys. Chaps of all shapes and sizes were Dad's Elephant Army in suits and bowler hats with rubber trunks, and ladies in leopard skin costumes were very real cheetahs and big cats. Behind the scenes wee dozens of helpers, stage managers, usherettes, make up artists, lighting engineers, programme sellers and all the rest, each and every one playing an essential role in making the whole programme run smoothly. It made me think.

With the rest of the world, I have watched the recent news of climate disasters, political feuds, foreign wars and increasingly decadent behaviour amongst the young with increasing alarm and despondency, wondering what we can do, where shall we go, how can we help and why are things going so wrong?

First, we can team up with others (united we stand; divided we fall), express our concerns (wherever there are two or more gathered together, something is bound to happen), accept our limitations of time or expertise, but know that however small the offering, the sum of all the parts is substantial. Things are going wrong because we are tempted to lead busy lives of instant gratification, no account of cost and very little thought for the long-term future. It is not too late, though we must all act now, at home, in the street, at work or wherever, to have any chance of making a difference. Take part in a real-life pantomime. Feel free to boo and hiss and cheer, and oil those creaking wheels by picking up litter, writing letters, lending a hand or even just sitting quietly and asking God for guidance. We can't all be leaders but when the light at the end of the tunnel is an oncoming express train, it is time to act. Don't let the baddies win.

Be Still

I was having a bad day.

The sponge had sunk in the middle – wretched stove!
The washing had blown off the line – useless pegs!
Water came from the cold tap in a miserable dribble
– why had the plumber not finished his job?   My
supper sandwich was stale and the wine tasted like
vinegar! 'What next?' I asked myself.

I know – there had been devastating storms in
France; civil war goes on and on in Russia; sickness
and poverty abound; one of my neighbours had a fall
but I only knew when the Police came; another
neighbour was ill but her family were on the case …
So, MY problems were paramount, weren't they?
Nobody seemed to care. I sulked.

As midnight approached, I found myself on my
knees … adjusting the stopcock under the sink.
Through the sound of freely running fresh water, I
heard the still, small voice:

Be still, for the power of the Lord is moving in this place
He comes to cleanse and heal, to minister His grace.
No work too hard for Him, in faith receive from Him.
Be still for the power of the Lord is moving in this place[3].

Thank goodness He never gives up on us. I went to

---

[3] Dave Evans 1986 Thank You Music

bed, ashamed of my selfishness, comforted by his unconditional love and forgiveness, with the promise that I would try harder tomorrow.

Differences

We all go shopping but choose different stores to get the same sort of goods. If we all choose to travel to the same place, we may go by different modes of transport, take different routes with a different timescale but still arrive at the same destination.

On the way, we see different things, meet different people, make different decisions that result in different destines. If all does not go according to plan, that opens up different directions and life goes on – but differently.

Like my beloved Bristol Granny "sometimes I sits and thinks and sometimes I just sits". Quiet reflection is a gentle relaxation exercise that can well take care of long, dark winter nights and dreary days (always remembering there is glory in the grey).

I was recently thumbing through a box of small, faded black and white photographs and found one dated 1946 when I was nine years old and visiting an orphanage in Devon with my parents. They were planning to adopt a little girl, my age, called Denise who had apparently lost her family in the London blitz. It was all very exciting and arrangements were well advanced when everything changed as it was discovered that they had, in fact, survived and were looking for her. Sometime later, they were all reunited and life went on, but differently.

We never heard what happened. Exactly how things changed for me is hard to say, but I am confident that my main path and direction remained much the same. I often wonder about that little girl and pray that she grew up knowing happiness and the love of her birth family as I have done. If not, I hope she may be spared the knowledge that there once was a different home where, having chosen her, we were waiting with welcome arms.

November

"I really do NOT like this time of year!" How often have I heard people say November is the hardest time and how often have I agreed and disappeared at speed to be sad, alone. What a waste. This year I have made a late resolution and feel great excitement.

My dear little house, so loving and forgiving when I leave it for long periods, is getting some attention and loving it. The sweep was the first on the scene and poked his brushes up and up until they popped out of the chimney into a cloudless blue sky and made me want to sing like Mary Poppins. That night I happily lit a fire, watched the embers burning, thought of roasted chestnuts at my Granny's and felt glad about the winter coming.

A kind neighbour has resurrected an old card table for me so I can do a jigsaw or invite friends round for whist. My outdoor plants are coming inside much refreshed by their summer holiday whilst their empty pots are washed and stored ready for spring. It is all coming together.

I am aware how blessed I am and thank God daily for my busy life and the choices I am free to make, but sometimes feel despair and lack of purpose. That is when I stop, say prayers of admission, and always find an answer – not necessarily what I want to hear, but what is good for me!

Like last Monday morning when I woke to hear the wind howling and the rain beating on the window. As I turned over and snuggled under the duvet, thankful I did not have to go out, I felt a spiritual nudge, so compelling that I was suddenly on the move. Halfway through the day, the sun was shining almost as if God was showing me what I could have missed by feeling fed up. There really is a silver lining if we stop, look and listen. Then do something positive.

Happiness is the Art of Making a Bouquet with the Flowers within Reach

My world fell apart in October 1987 when my beloved husband of 26 years walked out and suddenly there was nothing left to live for. After a great deal of thought, I made elaborate plans to commit suicide, failing in the end only because the hosepipe was too small to fit over the car exhaust. I was angry with myself for such incompetence and lack of foresight.

The following years were a struggle, working seven days a week as a nurse left no time for worrying, wishing or praying. I was alone, independent, a solo survivor and needed no-one. The turning point came at Christmas 1994 when I was suddenly taken seriously ill and had major life saving surgery. I lay in hospital immobilised by machine and drug lines and (at last) listened to Jesus. "You could have died – now LIVE". Of course, He had been there all the time but I had chosen to ignore Him. I am sad but not sorry about my time in the wilderness for it has stood me in good stead. Each and every day I pray for grace, discernment and greater understanding and give thanks for the Lord's persistence.

No longer a failure, I just take longer to get things right.

JOY

Precious things come in small packages and J-O-Y is a gem waiting to be unwrapped. Jesus first, yourself last and others in the middle – Initially, crossword fans will understand.

Joy is a little word packed to capacity with potential, like a mustard seed or sherbet dab that, popped in your mouth, will burst forth with froth and bubble. It is a kind word that costs nothing, suddenly appearing like snowdrops in spring or lurking contentedly in the fond memories of a Granny's unconditional love, home cook and cuddles.

One year, having spent six splendid, sun-filled weeks with my beloved offspring in Australia, I flew back to the UK in time for Christmas (December is height of summer there when temperatures can reach 50 and not my idea of fun!). Knowing the transition would not be easy, and everyone here would be otherwise engaged, I deliberately booked into a motel on a busy Midland motorway junction. Clean, cosy, comfy and, with triple glazing, quiet. A perfect location for retreat and reflection within easy reach of Lichfield Cathedral, the National Memorial Arboretum and a friendly, canal side pub that served endless yummy food. Oh joy!

A few days later back home alone, I was surprised to be overwhelmed by a strange feeling of tumbling helplessly in a spiralling vortex of chocolate (it might have been mud, but I didn't like that idea) and I had visions of Alice in Nowhereland. There was no fear, but sense of awe and wonder as I took myself to bed that New Year's Eve. For the next week, I spent a lot, lived on the only food I fancied, porridge, and felt totally at peace.

On Epiphany Sunday, I woke up and decided to go to Evensong. Singing carols by candlelight in a packed church was a gentle re-introduction to the real world. A burst of joy.

Walking home in the gathering gloom with a hint of snow in the air and lights peeping out from houses I imagined heaving with happy families, my mind went blank like an empty attic. A passer-by was approaching, I know not age or gender, size or shape as all I remember is a wide smile and a brief nod as whoever it was disappeared into the dusk. At that moment, a switch flicked in my head and there were wings beneath my feet. Such is joy.

Hope

Hope is not just about health, wealth, creed or colour. It is about choosing to believe that nothing is impossible. It is about choosing to believe that, in any situation, there is a certain resolution; in any destruction there can be resurrection; in deepest grief the possibility of peace, acceptance and new birth. Hope is easier to sustain in the company of faith and trust as the one provided strong foundations in times of crippling doubt and the other the durability of patience and peace of mind. Starved of hope, despair swiftly devours the mind and destroys the body.

As a teenager I was constantly falling in love, sure that my dreams of a happy ever after life were just around the corner. Sniffy Snelling was a school friend, with pebble glasses, a runny nose and smelly, shabby clothes, hopeless at absolutely everything. I was his friend, certain that all I had to do was find the key to his heart and he would be my prince. Inevitably disappointed, as he was bullied and teased and I made no impression on the situation, I never gave up hope that things would improve and I never forgot him.

There was Geoff with impeccable manners who courteously carried my school satchel, always walked me safely home and whose knowledge on almost anything opened my eyes to a wider world, but whose colour and creed were not acceptable in 1950s Britain. Eventually our paths divided and hope in the future inevitably faded but I never forgot him.

Then there were film stars and sportsmen whose pictures adorned my bedroom wall as I hoped to meet them and for whom I would have walked on hot coals and swum with crocodiles. Later, when I was a student nurse in the Garrison Medway Towns, there were sailors with bell-bottom trousers and coats of navy blue; handsome soldiers with fast cars and airmen who promised to fly me to the moon. Hope and expectation constantly walked hand in hand despite the empty promises of telephone calls that never came, cancelled rendezvous and more heartbreak, until the day that I was unexpectedly whisked away on a blind date and all my dreams came true.

Now, as I prepare to be launched into my eighties, I have the time and inclination to mull over all that has happened in the years that have flown by. I can appreciate that it is the possibility of things that can be equally fulfilling, not the guaranteed best outcome of our thoughts and aspirations. The world may spin faster, eyes may grow dim and horizons may shrink, but allow hope to spring eternal and be assured, nothing is impossible.

Building Tomorrow at St Mark's

As a recently elected chapel warden, I have been surprised (shocked, if I am honest) at how my attitude to my Church has changed. No longer the indulgent maiden aunt, effortlessly floating around with gifts of time to spare or money to bridge that yawning gap twixt dwindling income and increasing expenditure. No longer simply the intensely proud God-mother intuitively involved in whimsically watching a precious charge struggling to make sense of the mysteries of the modern world. No longer philosophically accepting disappointments and distractions and at the same time, sharing confidences and absent-mindedly absorbing concerns that adults apparently find bothersome. Suddenly, I am a grown up and feel like an expectant parent faced with REAL responsibility and a very scary future. Suddenly, I must think sensible grown-up thoughts based on facts, reflected in prayer and shared n discussion, not acted on in a flurry of froth and bubble. Suddenly, I need to put pen to paper for discussion and proper project planning and try to understand how to prioritise maintenance and repairs. Suddenly, I need to be patient ...

So, where to start? First essential principle must be to SEE CLEARLY and value what we already have and be thankful for the legacy we are privileged to enjoy today, only there because of the generosity, determination and expert management of previous worshippers and benefactors. They too must have faced the agony of limited resources and manpower and soldiered on in faith. We will remember them. As a Church family, we have a duty to be watchful, courageous, mindful and involved, free to express our own ideas and opinions but open to suggestions that mean change which is challenging but possibly necessary in the long term.

How can we increase the profile of our beautiful building for new audiences and future families to enjoy? Why have so many of our neighbours never set foot inside our Church, even on weekdays? What is the point of hiding beautiful glass panels, securely locked in darkness behind heavy oak doors? Are there ways we can encourage a wider ownership f the building by inviting outsiders to take an interest or shall we just stay as we are, in our holy huddle, safe and insulated, do nothing and risk suddenly losing absolutely everything that has taken so much to achieve?

It is up to us as guardians to do our best to do our duty to God and the Queen.

No Quick Fix

I have always had an ambivalent attitude to the concept of healing, convinced of divine intervention on one hand but with reservations about some human claims of solo success. I specially recall an experience in 1955 when, as an 18-year-old student, I was nursing a lad of the same age, who had been so badly injured he was expected to die. Whenever, I passed his bed, or tended to his battered body, I prayed for his peace and deliverance whilst not having the least idea what that meant in practical terms. After weeks of being in a deep coma and with no ventilators or modern drugs to rely on, he made a total recovery, later saying that he had found an inner strength. I knew something remarkable had happened but did not realise this was something I could build on.

Thirty-five years later, extremely vulnerable as a solo survivor desperately seeking comfort for a broken heart, I found myself on more than one occasion at the Birmingham National Exhibition Centre not far from where I was living at the time. Together with thousands of other people, I was transfixed by a figure in the far distance as he paced up and down on the stage. Shouting what sounded like unintelligible gobbledygook into a microphone, arms flailing, eyes a-popping, he soon whipped his audience into a frenzy. Buckets were frequently passed round by muscle-bound minders with fierce faces and in luminous uniforms. People absent-mindedly threw money in. Sticks and crutches ended up abandoned in piles, wheelchairs were discarded and pain and all disability apparently vanished. Tempting though this was, I was not impressed by the hysteria and empty rhetoric. It seemed too good to be true (and was, of course).

Like a hamster on a wheel, I was constantly running to keep still. Sleep only came as the result of absolute exhaustion and waking to a new day presented what I perceived to be a wretched and meaningless existence. An enormous black hole loomed large, reaching to infinity and beyond and, more than once, I was tempted to jump in, to find freedom. Nobody knew, but something always stopped me. For two years I battled on, working two jobs seven days a week, before, at last going to my GP with what I thought was a sensible solution and asked for a plastic bag for my head and a draw-string for my neck. He gently declined and we talked. At first it was like uncorking a bottle of fizzy pop and releasing the bubbles. Then reality set in. There was no quick fix.

With a lot of help and over time, I began to see that big black hole as much less fearful. It was somewhere to explore; it spelt adventure. It took the shape of the empty tomb and I discovered discarded remnants and real evidence of the life I thought I had lost. Familiar smells, music, letters, postcards, pictures, artefacts and books materialised, were scanned or carefully scrutinised, filed under "not needed on voyage" or stored for future reference.

Far from shrinking, my horizons were expanding and exciting, everything looked clear and different. I learnt to separate immediate needs from things that could wait. When in the middle of the night I discovered the bathroom flooded and water rising, I plugged the leak, switched off the mains, mopped up as much as possible and waited for morning to ring the plumber to say "I am not drowning, but I do need help". He came, but it was many weeks before things dried out and order was restored.

Healing comes in many shapes and situations but nothing worthwhile is gained in a hurry. Hiccups are inevitable and patience is essential. With the power of positive thinking and God's help, anything is possible. Believe me, I know!

Life or Death

Much is currently being bandied about in the press and, probably privately behind closed doors, about euthanasia. It generates all sorts of emotions, often shock and horror but also bewilderment and sometimes secret admiration for courage. Overall, we are left with far more questions than answers, but we have a duty to address this important issue if only to clear the attics of our minds in an honest attempt to understand what is at stake.

In 1987 I was fifty years old with three grown-up children launched happily on their very varied and independent lives across the world when my beloved husband, without warning, walked out to a new life and has not been in touch with the family since. Had he died, the effect would have been the same: total devastation and heartbreak but at least I could have laid him out, taken my leave and, hopefully, in time, moved on in peace with thanksgiving. As it was, the pain was unbearable and the future a black hole: a sentence without any possibility of parole or hope of remission. Had assisted suicide been available in any form, whatever the cost, I would have made full use of it.

Instead, I meticulously arranged my own demise which, mercifully, failed when I found the only hosepipe I had was too small to fit on the exhaust of my cosy, warm, fume-filled car in the hermetically sealed garage attached to our house.

This added to my overwhelming sense of failure (why else had I been rejected) and I isolated myself socially which, as I was living in a city suburb where the neighbours were anonymous commuters, was not difficult. Nobody noticed. I worked seven days a week at two jobs for several years until my health gave up and I had to give in.

I specially remember the disappointment of waking up after life-saving surgery, in hospital instead of Heaven where I longed to be. There was no pain but I was inelegantly tethered to the bed by tubes and machines and before I had time to protest at the indignity of it all, I heard a man's deep, gentle voice say "You could have died, now live!".

The room was empty.

In retrospect, I know that Jesus had been by my side every step of the way but I was too wrapped up in my own misery to listen. He finally got through and I am glad. Almost every day a small miracle happens that reminds me of the sanctity of life, and perhaps we should all be reminded of Christ's suffering on the cross before electing to take selfish advantage of being released from our own.

Light a Penny Candle

In *A Monk's Alphabet: Moments of Stillness in a Turning World* by Jeremy Driscoll we read:

What is so shocking about the present course of human history is that there is no longer operative any principle of unity. Countless thoughts – a good many of them noble and true and sincere – lie scattered over the face of the earth but with no force to pull them together …

Amen to that! In so many places there are people with their own agendas who either are incapable or unwilling to share, co-operate, or communicate with others. Hence a ragged and wretched and often expensive state of muddling through in incompetence and ineptitude. There is a territorial imperative, a fear of being overlooked or losing control; overwhelming desire for wealth and fame never mind the penalty. A selfishness, disregard for the consequences and ignorance of the effects we have on each other. Discernment is most difficult. It is a constant battle that we must all address, particularly looking outside the intimate holy huddles that make us feel safe and invulnerable.

The winter months are an ideal opportunity to shine light in dark corners. Listen carefully to the wind and lashing rain. See the changes. Hear things that go bump in the night. Have no fear. Lighten the darkness. A lot of penny candles could make all the difference and cost no more than setting aside a time of regular reflection and a willingness to take risks. Step out in faith. Let go. Accept change. You are not alone.

Neglected – and at risk

Despite political posturing, plenty of publicity and profound promises from PCHTs or their current metamorphosis, hospital patients continue to be neglected and put at risk.

On Christmas Eve, a 92-year-old friend of mine was admitted to Gloucester Royal Hospital with a fractured pelvis following a fall. On Boxing Day, visitors were shocked to find him unusually confused and dangerously dehydrated with several untouched drinks placed tantalisingly out of reach on the bedside table. Help came from the only member of staff on the ward who, when asked for assistance, quickly, kindly and without fuss, responded by putting up an IV drip. A doctor, presumably, but in the absence of formal identification, who knows. Where were the nurses providing continuity of care and reassurance to the vulnerable? Nowhere to be seen. What might have happened if the visitors had not intervened?

At the same time, staff at Henlow Court, a centre of excellence in Dursley which specialises in end-of-life care, were waiting to welcome back a very frail 90-year-old resident who, due to great pain, had been referred to casualty for a precautionary X-ray. However, as there was nobody to "sign her off" for discharge she had to stay in hospital over the weekend, with time to develop bed sores or pickup an infection. All she wanted was to be back in familiar surroundings with people she knew. Her distress and frustration were heart-breaking.

For heaven's sake! Patients are people not neat parcels to be matched and dispatched according to a system absolutely flawed, often thoughtless and even needlessly life-threatening.

In all the current rhetoric, I have not heard one brave person mention fundamental, essential and immediate changes so obviously needed in nurse training. A return to a clear apprentice career structure that embraces, celebrates and realistically rewards everyone from the named ward maid in charge of and accountable for standards of cleanliness on her own designated ward (not flitting between six) to junior nurses concentrating on comfort, feeding, bathing, toileting and mobilising patients, thus allowing those senior and experienced staff time for supervision, development and training in caring for more complicated cases.

I never had any difficulty in making good nurses from keen, caring young people from all backgrounds of education who wanted to learn on the job. Postgraduate nurses I preferred to leave at the ward door, encouraging them to develop their academic skills elsewhere, preferably far away from sick patients.

Please somebody – ditch Project 2000 and start again now.

A Pilgrimage to Lindisfarne May 2009

It was like standing on a launch pad waiting for someone to light the blue touch paper. We had been to preparation meetings, discussed arrangements and received instructions. At last, the great day dawned and space beckoned. The train journey from Cam and Dursley to Berwick on Tweed with only a change at Cheltenham was easy and the start of a voyage of discovering myself.

Lindisfarne, also known as Holy Island, lies two kilometres off the Northumberland coast in North East England, tenuously attached to the mainland by a narrow, metalled causeway a bit like an umbilical cord, which twice a day is covered by the tide to a depth of several feet. Day trippers are constantly watching the clock for fear of being stranded, so staying for a week was very special, with a curious sense of timelessness and isolation. Being of the world but not in it.

We were a party of about forty pilgrims from Dursley and district, based in cottages around the village and led in a varied programme of Retreat experiences by the resident Spiritual Director at St Cuthbert's Centre, Rev. Barry Hutchinson. Each day began formally, all of us together at 9.15 a.m. for morning prayer (sometimes twenty minutes silence which was new for me, but soon became compelling). This was followed by a Biblical reflection and meditation by various techniques which were simple to grasp and very effective. In the evenings after supper, we gathered again for prayers and a bedtime story told by Rev. Simon Helme, informative, thought provoking and fun.

The island embraces an extraordinary range of geography, animal, vegetable and mineral, from the northern landscape of brawling, shifting sand dunes knitted together by clumps of marram grass to the treacherous outcrop of rocks particularly famous for the daring rescue by Grace Darling and her father in 1838 of the shipwrecked crew and passengers from the SS Forfarshire. There are magnificent golden beaches and long country walks; a not very pretty castle perched like a pimple on a drum which was originally built as a fort in the 16th century and from the tiny harbour we took a small boat to the Farne Islands to see the plethora of sea birds: puffins, eider ducks, kittiwakes and cormorants to name but a few. And, of course, there were colonies of assorted seals, sunning themselves on the sand or playing round the boat. On other days, conducted prayer walks were an opportunity to hear more details about the history of the place and people. Time to ponder, in quiet company, one's own thoughts; to be in awe at the privilege of being there and free to give thanks whilst bathed in peace and tranquillity.

A church historian spent one whole morning talking about the Celtic saints and we also heard from a Franciscan Brother about modern monasticism, both illuminating, inspiring, interesting and entertaining. Catering was individual for each household; we shared some meals as a whole group and visited each other's places for informal chats over tea and coffee, getting to know people we had never met or knew only by sight or just casual acquaintances from Church back home.

There was plenty of time to wander further afield with Edinburgh, Alnwick and Hadrian's Wall not far away. One young family had great fun flying a kite in near gale force winds on the beach. Personally, I found the week extraordinarily unique. Hearing and learning about the past and the wonderful legacy handed down by those who had such courage and faith. Learning about myself by using the present in constructive silence and stillness of body and mind, but above all, learning to look forward confident that I am a little better equipped to hear God's word though the clamour of our busy world.

We were yesterday's children building castles in the sand. Now we're building tomorrow, the future's in our hands!

Jennifer with brother Brian on the beach

About the Editor:

Patricia Main began life in London's East End in an era before it became fashionable and has an enduring love for the City (especially in its Early Modern manifestation) despite spending most of her life in the South West of England. When not researching history for publication or editing texts written by others, she writes fiction.

You can find her on Facebook – **Patricia Ainger – Writer**. And now has a website (very much a work in progress) – **www.patricia.ainger.com**. She loves to hear from readers and always replies to any messages she receives.

Printed in Great Britain
by Amazon

72747060R00159